NAVIGATING THE COMPLEXITIES OF PRIVACY

NAVIGATING THE COMPLEXITIES OF PRIVACY

ISSUES FOR LIBRARIES AND CONTENT PROVIDERS

EDITED BY
DOREEN BRADLEY AND
HEATHER STAINES

Published in the United States of America by
ATG LLC (Media)
Manufactured in the United States of America

DOI: doi.org/10.3998/mpub.14413329

ISBN 978-1-941269-71-8 (print)
ISBN 978-1-941269-72-5 (ebook)

http://against-the-grain.com

CONTENTS

INTRODUCTION

Doreen Bradley and Heather Staines

Our interest in compiling this collection emerged from the growing interest in privacy across the scholarly communications ecosystem at multiple professional conferences. We were also fortunate to guest edit a special issue of *Serials Librarian* in 2021 through which we gathered many of our contributors. Early investigations concerning privacy and physical libraries may have seemed to be more of a local issue centering around what materials were checked out or what questions were posed to the reference desk. As digital access becomes the norm, complexities correspondingly arise around privacy and networked resources, data security measures, and shared services. New information systems evolve to meet the growing expectations of library users and library staff. In this new world with so much research, teaching, and learning activities happening online, the topic continues to grow in significance.

When we examine issues of the library management system (LMS) and third-party software, authentication, individualized services, learning analytics, and data sharing, issues quickly move beyond the local to the national or global level. Local state and national laws combine with evolving professional guidelines. Library boards, directors, staff, users, vendors, researchers, students, faculty and institutions, just to name a few, all have perspectives which are important elements of the ongoing conversation. As

Brian Watson notes in a Library Privacy Primer (https://americanlibraries magazine.org/blogs/the-scoop/library-privacy-primer/), there is no right to privacy in the Constitution; it actually originates from the 1965 *Griswold v. Connecticut* Supreme Court ruling—one in the news quite often recently after the overturning of *Roe v Wade*. Another key development stems from concerns around the 2001 Patriot Act which broadened data collection on US citizens on national security grounds. The revitalized conversation around social justice and equity that followed the murder of George Floyd and so many others has also influenced the ongoing discourse on privacy issues, in terms of which voices have a chance to be heard and what others might not yet be represented.

We cast a wide net in identifying articles that would illustrate the expansive discussion on privacy in libraries, from practical issues to theoretical discourses. While the large discussions of cloud-based tools, authentication, and network security often capture our attention, there are many issues that are individualized to the local library level, such as staff training protocols and institutional policies regarding access and ownership of data. With this collection we hope to present a range of interviews, columns, and research articles that cover new ideas and highlight nuances in important and ongoing discussions to advance our professional conversations around privacy. We acknowledge that many aspects of patron privacy are not addressed in this collection. Certainly, patrons are not a monolithic block, and we see on a daily basis laws proposed and passed that target vulnerable and marginalized populations such as LGBTQ+ individuals. We hope that a future volume might be allotted to exploring these important developments more fully.

As users prioritize ease of access to library resources from anywhere they choose to work, data security will continue to be an issue. Privacy and personal data management are quickly becoming new facets of information literacy, and libraries are responding with educational programs to aid in understanding these issues. Libraries, themselves, are learning how to mitigate the risks through better policies and education of key stakeholders, and new technologies enable users to better safeguard their data. Navigating the perspectives and values of librarians, researchers, and vendors when it comes to personal information and data is an ongoing challenge. It may be that issues as fundamental as *who has access to data?*, *for what purposes can this data be used?*, or even *who owns library data?*, will dominate this conversation, particularly in the new AI era.

This project took longer than originally intended, due in part to the COVID-19 pandemic, which highlighted specific privacy issues in communication with authors and editors, or our own challenges in crafting this title from a variety of remote locations. We want to thank our editor, Matthew Ismail, our peer reviewers, and our contributors who made a special effort in a time of uncertainty. Their hard work has truly improved the quality of this project.

CHAPTER 1

PRIVACY AND "GREY DATA" IN LIBRARY SYSTEMS

A Case Study

Cristina Colquhoun, Clarke Iakovakis, Megan Macken, Nikhil Motwani, and Damith Perera

INTRODUCTION

This chapter will explore privacy issues related to *grey data* in university libraries. The term *grey data*, coined by Christine Borgman, describes "the vast array of data that universities accumulate outside the research realm," generated by and about individuals "in their daily activities of research, teaching, learning, services, and administration" (2018, p. 380). Academic libraries, which are centralized, discipline-agnostic, and part of a global network of information providers, can offer their universities an essential service: vital, critical assessment of information systems that produce grey data.

The chapter is not intended to be prescriptive, but rather to offer a case study of library-led efforts at Oklahoma State University (OSU) to advocate for personal data privacy and advance those same practices for grey data in their own libraries. Specifically, the authors will share their local experience adopting new applications or systems, sharing archival data, developing local applications, and advocating for and educating the university community about privacy in terms of grey data. OSU Libraries and the institution at large do not view the use of data analytics as a violation of privacy, per se, but realize that they should use the data within certain ethical guidelines and with as much user consent as is possible. This is especially important as libraries venture into newer areas such as research information management or linked open data for archival materials of living people.

Additionally, libraries may also integrate their resources and services into other systems, such as learning management platforms, or develop local applications that may not garner as much scrutiny in matters of privacy as enterprise-scale systems.

LITERATURE REVIEW: PRIVACY AND GREY DATA IN LIBRARIES

A Vocational Imperative

In recent librarianship, the use of data to demonstrate library value has come into laser focus. The Association of College and Research Libraries' (ACRL) 2010 commissioned report, *The Value of Academic Libraries*, called on libraries to provide data showcasing their value toward institutional success and quality (Oakleaf, 2010). Since this report, much scholarship has emerged on the topic, as well as urgent calls to understand the ethics of data use and its effect on patron privacy. The patron right to privacy and confidentiality is an issue that has been codified into various library standards of practice (American Library Association [ALA], 2019a, 2021a; National Information Standards Organization [NISO], 2015). For example, the Library Bill of Rights Article VII affirms the right of all people to privacy and exhorts libraries to "advocate for, educate about, and protect people's privacy" (ALA, 2019a). ALA further states that privacy is "necessary for intellectual freedom" and is "fundamental to the ethical practice of librarianship" (ALA, 2019b, para. 15). ALA has developed an ethical framework and comprehensive primer on privacy in libraries from the perspective of both intellectual freedom and advocacy (ALA, 2021b). ALA also provides a resource on applicable state laws governing libraries and privacy (ALA, 2021c). For an introduction to practical privacy matters and a broad overview of practical approaches to privacy in the library, see *Library Patrons' Privacy: Questions and Answers* (Valenti et al., 2022).

Local Policies

Mechanisms that offer protection for patron privacy will vary by state laws as well as by institutional and individual library governance policies. As Borgman (2018) warns, however, "Governance mechanisms to assure protection of privacy, academic freedom, intellectual property, information security, and compliance with regulations in the uses of such data are nascent, at best" (p. 371). For example, Oklahoma §65-1-105 protects patron data by requiring a court order or patron authorization for its dissemination by public libraries (Oklahoma Statute 65, 2013). This law covers requests for data from individuals, but does not address the many systems that convey and connect patron data from multiple sources. In 2023, the Oklahoma House of Representatives passed the Oklahoma Computer Data Privacy Act (2023), a bill based on the California Consumer Privacy Act (CCPA) that would require consumers to opt in to data collection (Stauss, 2022), but it stalled in the state senate (where a similar law failed to pass in 2021 and 2022). The passing of such a law would take a step toward protecting grey data by making data sharing explicit and by giving consumers some control over their personal or grey data. Connecticut, Virginia, Colorado, and Utah have successfully legislated such measures (Lively, 2022).

Beyond state laws, institutional privacy and data governance policies and plans typically provide overarching rules for any institutional data use. While there is guidance and precedent for developing these policies, Borgman (2018) highlights that more is needed to adequately protect patrons:

> Tenets of privacy by design, the Code of Fair Information Practice, the Belmont Report, and codifications of academic and intellectual freedom are established and tested. Implementation is often incomplete, however. For faculty, students, staff, research subjects, patients, and other members of the university community to enjoy protection of information and autonomy privacy, more comprehensive enforcement of principles such as limiting data collection, ensuring data quality, and constraining the purposes for each data element is necessary.
>
> (p. 410)

Additionally, privacy and data governance policies written for the institution as a whole are often inadequate to extend to the needs of individual departments such as the academic library. For example, OSU's *Privacy Notice* (2017) applies to all OSU Library patrons who use any Library websites and web services, and OSU's *Data Stewardship* policy (2019) applies to all Library employees who may handle data. However, there is a lack of specificity in how these policies and procedures apply to data produced and/or collected with library services and vendors, and libraries have a duty to protect users' privacy and rights beyond what is required by law or policy. There is a need for individualized, robust policies and frameworks specific to each library and their patron population (Briney, 2019; Jones & Salo, 2018).

Although a number of academic libraries have taken concrete action by codifying privacy statements and policies (Auraria Library, 2020; Indiana University Libraries, 2012; Nichols Hess et al., 2015; Stanford Libraries, n.d.; University of Michigan Information and Technology Services, n.d.; Zoss et al., 2021), Jones, Briney, et al. (2020) note much work still needs to be done at the local library policy and governance levels. Efforts such as the Licensing Privacy Project (Hinchliffe, n.d.), among others, have produced guidelines and resources for libraries in drafting privacy and governance policies (Cooper, 2021; Heller & Galvan, 2020; Intellectual Freedom Committee, 2020; LDH Consulting Services, 2022). An analysis of the privacy policies published online by US libraries as an ALA Tech Report covers systems and integrations as well as data security and retention (Vaughan, 2020).

Technical Considerations for Privacy

While the ideal of privacy is fundamental to librarianship, the wide range of library systems that interconnect with each other and with non-library applications complicate privacy in practice. Scholars have noted frequent gaps and inadequate language used within vendor policies and terms of service that create potential threats to patron privacy and security as well as infringe on librarian ethical codes (Asher et al., 2018; Hanson, 2019; McKinnon & Turp, 2022; Paris et al., 2021). The Privacy and Ethics in Technology Working Group of the Digital Library Federation has developed guidance for library-built systems and data, including a user data risk assessment (Briney et al., 2020). Additionally, Briney's (2019) critical review of library data management practices recommends security improvements that most libraries need to implement to protect student data privacy, especially for data anonymization.

These technical considerations are essential; libraries that are not "proactively enabling user privacy features may have unwittingly violated the principles of user privacy expressed by the ALA, CNI, NISO and IFLA privacy guidelines" (O'Brien et al., 2018, p. 736). O'Brien et al.'s (2018) study offers practical advice for configuring Google Analytics on academic library websites. For applications adopted widely outside of libraries, for example, third-party integrations or skill development for voice-based assistants, literature in adjacent fields such as human–computer interaction and other information technology fields can provide practical guidance both relevant to libraries and accessible to non-specialists (Lentzsch et al., 2021; Utz et al., 2022). These are particularly relevant for library applications that facilitate patrons' access to resources but encroach on their privacy. Many research databases and digital scholarship platforms offer Google login and file storage. Salo (2021) suggests the concept of physical-equivalent privacy, where librarians compare an e-resource with the level of privacy offered through its physical equivalent as a gauge of the privacy offered to patrons. David Irvin (2021) envisions a library "where critical information flows in, but very little if any 'digital exhaust' escapes it" (p. 35) through strict information security protocols.

While these comparisons are useful for print surrogates, they are more difficult to replicate as libraries adopt new roles and technology advances. Mobile apps, including those from e-book vendors or for campus history tours, may access personal data such as location, social networks, photos, contacts, etc.; a basic how-to privacy guide for app users is available from the Federal Trade Commission (FTC, 2021).

Advocating for and Educating the University Community

Given librarians' specialized knowledge of information and data, their ethical codes of practice, and unique placement within institutions, library and information science (LIS) scholars have framed librarians as necessary advocates for ethical data use within and across institutions (Doty, 2020; Jones & Salo, 2018; Oakleaf, 2016; Oakleaf et al., 2017). Some adamantly disagree, however, and view data involvement as an ethical issue in which librarians should not engage, while others believe librarians cannot afford to be excluded from the institutional data conversation, arguing that it would cost them "a seat at the [institutional] table" (Jones, 2019, p. 419). Jones (2019) makes the case for an ethical data middle ground, but one that first requires further training of LIS professionals in data methods and ethics.

Several initiatives have functioned to prepare academic librarians for ethical data governance, practice, and institutional advocacy. For instance, training opportunities and materials offered through Library Freedom's Crash Courses (n.d.), the Prioritizing Privacy program (Hinchliffe & Jones, n.d.), and Penn State University Libraries' Privacy Workshop series (Chisholm & Hartman-Caverly, 2021; Hartman-Caverly & Chisholm, 2021a, 2021b). Additionally, documentation produced by various groups has been instrumental in providing practical guidance for data use (ALA, n.d.; Asher et al., 2018; Bettinger et al., 2019; Briney et al., 2020; Value in Academic Libraries' Subcommittee on Learning Analytics and Privacy, 2021; Young et al., 2019).

One area of increasing importance that falls within the purview of libraries is the teaching of privacy literacy (Hartman-Caverly & Chisholm, 2020). A growing number of resources are available to help librarians become effective privacy literacy educators as well as provide curricula for privacy literacy sessions (Caines, n.d.; Chisholm & Hartman-Caverly, 2018, 2022; Electronic Frontier Foundation, n.d.; Lewis et al., 2018; University of California San Diego, n.d.; Walker et al., 2019). Additionally, scholars have created privacy literacy frameworks for teaching and researching privacy literacy (Kumar & Byrne, 2022; Rotman, 2009; Trepte et al., 2015).

PATRON CONCERN FOR DATA PRIVACY

Student and Faculty Views on Data Privacy

It is clear that data privacy measures are advocated not only by professional organizations and legislatures, but also by the patrons themselves. A variety of recent studies conclude that students and faculty are invested in their data privacy (Asher et al., 2022; Jones, 2019; Jones, Asher, et al., 2020; Jones et al., 2022; Li et al., 2021; Luzeckyj et al., 2020; Slade et al., 2019). Research suggests that, contrary to commonly held beliefs, many students do care about their data. Students want to be involved in decisions about their data, but don't always know who has access to it or why or what choices they have. They want to have a say and be heard, but they often feel powerless (Jones, Asher, et al., 2020). Students trust libraries when it comes to their data (Jones et al., 2019). Students trust their schools more than they trust corporations. Students see their schools as "moral" (Jones, Asher, et al., 2020, p. 17) because they aren't trying to make money off of them, but rather act in the students' best interest, and therefore they trust these institutions more with their data.

Students provide their data because they trust that their schools will use it to benefit students.

There are knowledge gaps when it comes to students and student data privacy literacy, which affects their ability to make informed decisions (Jones et al., 2019; Jones, Asher, et al., 2020). Students take issue with their institutions sharing their data with third parties, but are more comfortable with it when there is transparency regarding how and why the data is used, when they are offered choices with their data use, and when identifying information is stripped out (Jones et al., 2019).

Student Data Privacy

An abundance of literature from privacy scholars and practitioners provides guidance on measures that protect student data privacy. Grey data that is specific to teaching and learning is referred to as learning analytics (LA). LA is data about learners and their learning environments that we can use to understand and improve their learning experiences (International Learning Analytics & Knowledge Conference, 2010). LA scholarship is highly relevant for library systems, which integrate with student learning platforms and student information systems. The idea of the university as a trusted data steward or "information fiduciary" urges data practices that (i) advance student interests, (ii) support the educational mission of the institution, (iii) use data only when doing so is consistent with principles of intellectual freedom, and (iv) use data only in a way that is consistent with profound trust between student and institution (Jones, Rubel, et al., 2020, p. 1237; see also Balkin, 2016).

Ethical principles of transparency, agency, anonymization, and accountability for LA privacy (NISO, 2015; Pardo & Siemens, 2014; Prinsloo & Slade, 2013) could likewise be applied to other student data in library systems. Roberts et al. (2017, p. 104, Table 7.2) have developed a matrix for exploring the impact of LA on stakeholders throughout a university that could be repurposed for other types of data collection in libraries. Drachsler and Greller's (2016) checklist for developing ethical LA, known as "DELICATE," asks, "Why are you allowed to have the data?" (p. 96). Kurzweil and Stevens (2018) offer a unique perspective for working together with vendors on a responsible approach to privacy. Examples of LA policies in practice are available from the University of California Berkeley (n.d.), the University of Hawaii at Manoa (2018), and the Open University (n.d.). As Borgman (2018) notes,

> Data practices, privacy, academic and intellectual freedom, intellectual property, trust, and stewardship all are moving targets. Principles live longer than do the practices necessary to implement those principles...By encouraging each individual to focus on uses of data, the problem becomes personal.
>
> (p. 411)

OSU's efforts to follow this guidance are detailed below in a case study, focusing on privacy and grey data in platforms and software services, systems and server administration, and application development. We are not covering privacy issues that are well documented elsewhere, choosing to bring attention to more recent, unique "uses of data" not specifically covered in the literature (Borgman, 2018, p. 411).

CASE STUDY: GREY DATA AT OSU

Web-Based Software

Learning Management Platforms

One area where libraries may heavily encounter grey data is LA within library instruction. LA data can include the intellectual property students produce as well as the data they produce in the process of creating and using digital environments for learning. There are a plethora of third-party, digital tools available to assist in the process of library teaching, learning, and assessment, many of which produce LA in a variety of ways. In libraries, the most ubiquitous tools are SpringShare's LibGuides, learning management systems (LMSs), and other third-party applications, many offered via Learning Tools Interoperability (LTI) integration into the LMS. Although third-party tools are considered extensions of educational institutions and therefore still accountable under the Family Educational Rights and Privacy Act (FERPA, 2011), legal requirements are severely lacking in their ability to fully protect students and their data, especially when it comes to the potential for data commodification (Rhoades, 2020; Russell et al., 2018; Zeide, 2016, 2017).

Data leaks and the sale of major educational technology vendors (including all of their student data) are two factors that have increased public outcry for transparent and clear student data protections. For example, the sale of the company Instructure (best known for its LMS product, Canvas) in 2019 to a private equity firm kicked off a coordinated campaign of concerned stakeholders led by librarians (Young, 2020).

Recognizing the multifaceted potential for student harm in using LA, the Library Teaching and Learning team at OSU Libraries took Collier's (2017) challenge "to recognize and deconstruct our perspectives on the relationship of data to our understanding of student learning" (p. 56). Following the lead of privacy scholars and practitioners, the team of faculty librarians—led by the Instructional Design and Online Learning Librarian and composed of instruction and liaison librarians, the coordinator of OpenOKState (the University's open educational resource (OER) program), and the director of Library Teaching and Learning—formed a foundational, ethical, and epistemological stance on student data privacy that led to the development of a set of guiding principles. Using these principles, they created the Student Data Privacy Guidelines for collecting and using students' LA data (OSU Library Teaching & Learning, 2021). The plan not only seeks to respect and protect privacy, but also enables students to make educated, information-literate decisions about their data, respects their autonomy and intellectual rights, and helps build a trust relationship between them and the library. With each round of development, the team sought feedback from students and edited the content accordingly. For more in-depth details on the guidelines as well as the team's process, see Colquhoun et al. (2021).

Google Analytics

Most websites and library applications use Google Analytics since it is a free, powerful suite of tools that gives insight about users to site owners. Many times "free" equates to commodification of students' data in exchange for a product. In offering free and reduced-cost educational materials, OSU Libraries strive to do so without such an exchange of goods. This commitment becomes more difficult to carry out when systems like Google Analytics cross platforms. In Analytics, website domain(s) are added to the platform, data about website visitors and their site activity is collected and analyzed by Google, and then it is delivered to the website owner on an interactive dashboard. Google Analytics collects the user's IP address, location, operating system version, and type of web browser. With a custom implementation or in combination with other products such as Ads or Tag Manager, it can also collect and combine data about the user's app activity, text or telephone conversation, point-of-sale transactions data, and other personal information. Google Analytics also capitalizes on users' cookies, which store information about users and their searching behavior on the internet, to gather information about them (for more information about cookies, see also Valenti et al., 2022).

This causes concern because the user's personal information and activities are gathered without their consent and they are tracked and targeted. According to O'Brien et al. (2018), a majority of libraries have https enabled, but most do not use IP anonymization for Google Analytics. Upon review, this was also the case for two instances of Analytics in use for OSU Libraries, and we followed O'Brien's steps for anonymizing the IP address of site visitors. Additionally, we recently used Google Analytics data to inform the restructuring of the library website. The Analytics dashboard clearly delineated the most and least frequently visited pages and identified visitors' paths through the website. Neither user IP addresses nor the consumer habits of particular visitors would have provided useful insight for a website redesign. Google does provide an opt-out option for users in the form of its Opt-out Browser Add-on (Google, 2023). Albeit, a prerequisite to taking advantage of this option is alerting users that the option exists and where to find it. It may also seem rather counterintuitive to users to install a product directly into a browser to avoid tracking in a browser by that same exact company.

Linked Open Data for Living People

One place grey data may occur is in library collections themselves. During the COVID-19 pandemic, many libraries began actively contributing to Wikidata (WikiProject, 2020). Data reuse is standard practice for bibliographic metadata, but may become problematic when the focus of the data is living people, such as faculty authors or archival agents, such as interviewees, donors, or subjects of photographs. A recent project at OSU examined the ethical implications of creating linked open data in Wikidata for the Oklahoma Native Artists Oral History Series (Oklahoma Oral History Research Program, 2022). The collection comprises interviews of Indigenous artists with a connection to the state of Oklahoma. The artists consented to the interviews and later most agreed to have Wikipedia profiles created for them by OSU. Additionally, the project portal promotes the artists by showcasing their photographs and individual websites. Wikidata is one avenue for expanding "notability" through citation, exhibition, and award data while increasing awareness of contemporary Native American art.

However, some artists may consent to being profiled on the library website, but not wish to appear at the top of a Google search in a prominent knowledge panel. Additionally, the Wikidata properties for ethnicity, citizenship, or gender/sexuality do not readily capture the nuances related to identity that artists may express in oral history interviews. Even if a conscientious cataloger omits these properties from Wikidata for this reason, another editor may "fill in the blanks" with less care and potentially cause harm to the subject of that data. For published authors, useful tools can transfer ORCID author data directly into Wikidata in a few clicks (see, for example, SourceMD, 2022). Again, privacy issues arise when Wikidata editors "fill in the blanks" by including personal data that the author has not consented to sharing on a public platform. Borgman (2018) firmly states that "notice and consent should never be implicit" (p. 410). Just because it is possible to find this grey data easily at one's institution or on a public search, does not imply consent to sharing it. In one sense it is a name authority entry, which librarians have been creating for decades, but in another, very important sense, it is personal data that belongs to a human being rather than a library. The line dividing the two is not clear, but ethical guidelines help clarify the matter.

The Oklahoma Native Artists linked open data (LOD) project involves working directly with the artists to obtain consent for creating LOD profiles in Wikidata (or an alternate local LOD platform) on their behalf. Training on Wikidata is also offered to artists and their communities for creating Wikidata entries themselves. The library's decision to obtain consent stems from the Oral History Association Principles and Best Practices (Oral History Association, 2018) and the CARE Principles for Indigenous Data Governance (Research Data Alliance, 2019), which emphasize consent and centering the data owner. Additionally, the Markkula Center for Applied Ethical Toolkit provides excellent checklists for assessing motives prior to collecting data (Vallor et al., 2018). These exercises can help maintain ethical goals and improve transparency around data collection practices. For a description of the consent process and for more information about the project, see Macken et al. (2023).

Research Information Management (RIM) Systems

RIM systems provide a single source of data about faculty research and scholarship, typically gathered from internal and external databases and linked directly to individuals (see Bryant et al., 2021a for a more nuanced and elaborate definition). Data harvested from internal sources may derive from human resources (official and preferred names, start and leave dates, rank/title, department, and contact information), grants and financial awards (grant names, funders, and amounts), and the registrar (courses taught, number of students, and description).

External data includes bibliographic metadata related to scholarly and creative works, and scholarly identifiers (such as ORCID iDs). Finally, faculty may enter new data that is not present in any external or internal sources—or at least is not linked to them in a centralized location—such as employment history, biographical overview, research interests, degrees, affiliated websites (such as LinkedIn, Twitter, or personal websites), and service activities (such as board memberships, peer review activity, fellowships, media appearances, and community engagement work). Universities may implement RIM systems for a range of reasons, including to analyze research and publishing patterns (such as bibliometric analysis, co-authorship, topic modeling), to determine areas of interdisciplinary expertise and connect faculty across the university, to more efficiently meet mandatory reporting obligations, to build an online public profile system, and to manage the annual reporting and tenure and promotion process (Bryant et al., 2018, 2021a).

It is clear that gathering this data in a single database creates opportunities for researchers to more easily showcase their work and better connect with each other, external colleagues, funders, and members of the public. It also has the potential to greatly ease the labor burden on administrators, staff, and faculty to compile reports required for purposes such as accreditation and compliance with funder open access requirements. However, given that a significant amount of data is added to the system on behalf of individuals, awareness and efforts to protect user privacy must be central. A working group at the University of California system found privacy in RIM systems to be an "area of concern" among faculty and other stakeholders, asking if faculty are aware this information was being gathered on them and how it is being presented; who has access to the data (including entities outside the university, such as law enforcement and animal rights groups); and whether the companies collecting this data may have ulterior motives (University of California, 2021, p. 12). Nevertheless, they noted that managers of these systems "demonstrated clear understanding of faculty privacy and transparency concerns" (University of California, 2021, p. 29). Similarly, in a case study by OCLC Research, a RIM system administrator noted, "One of the surprises for me was the extent to which [protecting sensitive information] became an issue in our implementation" (Bryant et al., 2021b, p. 26).

The OSU Library has led the university-wide implementation of the Symplectic Elements RIM System, known locally as Experts Directory, and continues to serve as lead system administrator. During the ongoing configuration of this system, in which we customize the data structure to make the system more usable for OSU faculty, we have been actively "limiting data collection, ensuring data quality, and constraining the purposes for each data element" (Borgman, 2018, p. 46). This has been an iterative process dependent on open dialogue with faculty users, IT, HR, administrators, and among librarians on the project team. Particularly as we migrate data from another RIM system, we are able to ask if we really need this data point and if the data factors into accreditation and other reporting. Collecting less data not only promotes privacy, but simplifies the data entry process for faculty and streamlines the migration process for the project team.

Regardless of these efforts to collect less data and ensure sensitive data is not added to the system, the system may include information that individuals prefer to remain private or at least not to link to them on a public profile site, even if that data is available publicly online elsewhere. Borgman's (2018) warning to avoid implicit consent applies to RIM systems as well, and it is essential that the individual be able to see all data linked to them and have final say over what appears on their public profile. For instance, one researcher co-authored a paper with someone who became a target of online harassment and wished to hide that publication from their profile. Users may wish to keep certain grants from industry partners or in sensitive research areas private (Macken & Iakovakis, 2021, p. 95). If the system is being used for annual reviews, the researcher may wish to include relevant information about their activities that their reviewers can see but that they do not wish to appear on their public profile. The robust privacy controls that the system developers have programmed in allow users to select which data to make public, internal (i.e., visible only to other users logged in), or private.

While these privacy controls are becoming increasingly prevalent, we must acknowledge there are still legal and contractual obligations that can override individual preferences and the desire for certain information to be private. For instance, the so-called "Nelson Memo" issued by the White House Office of Science and Technology Policy (Nelson, 2022) stipulates that federal agencies must instruct funded researchers to "provide federal agencies with the metadata associated with all published research outputs they produce." Disclosure of this metadata, which includes author and co-author names, affiliations, and sources of funding, can be (and in some cases, is required to be) pushed from ORCID profiles, which are in turn often integrated with RIM systems. As another example, university administration and campus communication offices may, formally or informally, require faculty profiles to be made public as a means for recruiting students and communicating about the university's scholarship internally or to members of the public.

Privacy education has also been an integral part of our RIM system implementation. We developed a privacy guide that walks users through their options for sharing data publicly and offers transparency regarding third-party integrations. It also points to the RIM system vendor's profile on the Privacy Shield Framework, which is a useful starting point although it is no longer a "valid mechanism to comply with EU data protection requirements" (Privacy Shield, n.d., para. 2). While these are important steps, they do not fully address privacy concerns. For example, upgrades bring changes to the user interface, so maintaining the privacy guide with screenshots and detailed instructions is time consuming, as is checking to see if new third-party integrations have been implemented. While faculty opt in to sharing their profile publicly, they do not actively consent to any data collection by third parties.

During the procurement process for this platform, we referenced the *Scholarly Communications Infrastructure Checklist* and the recommendations of the SPARC Landscape Analysis, developing a set of questions related to privacy, information security, and data ownership (Aspesi, 2019; Feinstein et al., 2018; Macken & Iakovakis, 2021). As suggested above, Kurzweil and Stevens (2018) offer further guidance. Throughout implementation we have sought to balance the use of the data—to raise the research profile of faculty and to encourage open access sharing through the institutional repository integration—with empowering faculty to share or hide their data publicly, and privacy concerns related to data added on researchers' behalf. There are a number of additional critical privacy considerations not explored here, pertaining to a user's ability to opt out, the system's reinforcement of overreliance on uncontextualized metrics in annual reviews (such as journal-based citation metrics and quantity of articles published), and governing who has access to what data to run reports (Macken & Iakovakis, 2021).

Open Journal Systems (OJS)

OJS is a unique, open-source software by the Public Knowledge Project for organizing, reviewing, and publishing journals. Due to the challenging nature of migrating publications on this platform, libraries may have delayed important updates. Checking the application's underlying system requirements is important as some software versions could pose security threats. We share a specific experience with OJS version two as a cautionary tale about how system security impacts user privacy. This could occur in the future with different versions, platforms, or systems. OJS version two utilized PHP version four or earlier, which threatened the security of the application but was more reliable than PHP version five, which at the time possessed even more vulnerabilities. These vulnerabilities allowed the OSU implementation to be hacked, causing the following difficulties:

1. Account Creation by Bots: OJS 2.x didn't have any type of Captcha in place to differentiate new users from bots. This helped the hackers to

set up bots and create endless accounts on the applications, resulting in a crowded and slow database for querying.

2. Copyright Infringement: Due to the lack of security, the hackers were able to get access to the upload directory and were able to upload files and images to the server. There were incidents where hackers would copy copyright-protected images on the server's directory. We had to take down the URL for those images as that was considered Copyright Infringement under Section 512(c) of the Digital Millennium Copyright Act.
3. Defacement Attacks: OJS 2.x was very prone to defacement attacks as hackers were easily able to penetrate the front-end of the application and add or replace content. These messages and images had inappropriate content or a notice that it had been hacked by a specific person or group of hackers. This type of attack is generally done through SQL injection, Cross-site Scripting, DNS Hijacking, and Malware Injection.

While these are security concerns, when security is compromised, user privacy is at risk. OJS stores personal data such as user emails, addresses, and draft and rejected publications, as well as peer reviews and ratings, most of which are not intended for public consumption so consent has not been obtained to release that data. Upgrading to OJS version three resolved the three issues above and also includes a configurable privacy statement with required consent as part of the registration or submission process (Public Knowledge Project, 2018). The time-intensive migration process, however, could not be completed as quickly as the attacks warranted. To prevent future issues, in addition to updates, users' accounts are maintained with greater vigilance according to a set of parameters for unused accounts, including last login greater than three years ago; no login since initial account creation; no submissions or reviews in the system; or no institutional email or affiliation provided.

Server Administration

The servers that host these platforms can cause additional privacy concerns. Data security and privacy have become a major concern in the present IT world as they are the most important factors when choosing a vendor for Infrastructure as a Service. When opting for Cloud Computing, the data resides in the third party's storage location, which raises an alarm for privacy concerns. The applications which contain sensitive data and are hosted on the cloud using a third party's Virtual Machine infrastructure can be accessed easily from anywhere in the world if the vendor doesn't implement proper security measures.

Security measures that could help in securing the system and privacy of the data include the following:

1. Virtual Private Network (VPN) Enforcement: The vendor should impose the rules on IP accessibility in a way that it can only be accessed when connected to VPN. This technique can reduce the accessibility and reach of the server on the internet and thus will reduce attacks.
2. Secure Shell (SSH) Login: The user should implement SSH private and public keys for remotely accessing the servers.
3. Firewall: The vendor should put a firewall in place to filter out malicious traffic. This helps in building an extra layer of security on the servers and helps in securing the ports from which the servers can be accessed.
4. Web Interfaces/Application Programming Interfaces (APIs): The vendor should impose a two-factor authentication for accessing and managing the servers through the web interface.

There are various open-source content management applications like WordPress and Omeka that allow users to create and host websites. These applications should be updated regularly to the latest releases as they generally include security patches that help to avoid data breaches and strengthen the overall security of the applications. Some of the security concerns that we addressed are as follows:

1. Admin Panel URL: The URL for the admin panel is very easy to guess and hackers can easily gain access to the default login page, if not customized, by attempting a brute-force attack. In WordPress the

default login page for the admin panel has /wp-admin at the end of the domain name in the URL.

2. Security Plugins: Security plugins can provide additional security by enabling IP access control, reCAPTCHA, and two-factor authentication. They also provide a detailed analysis of the attack and blacklist the person or IP(s) from performing these attacks.
3. File Permissions and Ownership: The file permissions and ownership on the server should allow the website owner to access most of the data and provide limited access to the public.

APPLICATION DEVELOPMENT

Spaces Room Reservation System and Custom User Interface

OSU Library was using LibCal's "Room Booking" system for reserving study rooms. In the system, when users book a room, they should enter the name and email address manually. The system validates the email address is "okstate" email by checking the domain name (@okstate.edu). This presented a security issue because someone could book a room without having a valid okstate email address.

After Springshare updated their "Room Booking" to a system called "Spaces," they integrated user authentication with an external single sign-on (SSO) system. For example, at OSU we use Aperono CAS to process SSO, and Spaces integrated with the CAS system to authenticate. This integration makes reserving a room more secure by requiring a valid, authenticated username and password.

OSU Library developers created a local "Spaces-UI" front-end product to reserve study rooms on SpringShare's Spaces back-end. Spaces-UI successfully integrated with the OSU CAS system to provide the user authorization. By integrating both Spaces and Spaces-UI systems with CAS, patrons may more securely and easily reserve study rooms.

ILS (Alma) API, Collecting User Info from Student Information System

The Integrated Library System (ILS), ExLibris Alma is the platform OSU uses to manage print, electronic, and digital materials. Alma provides many

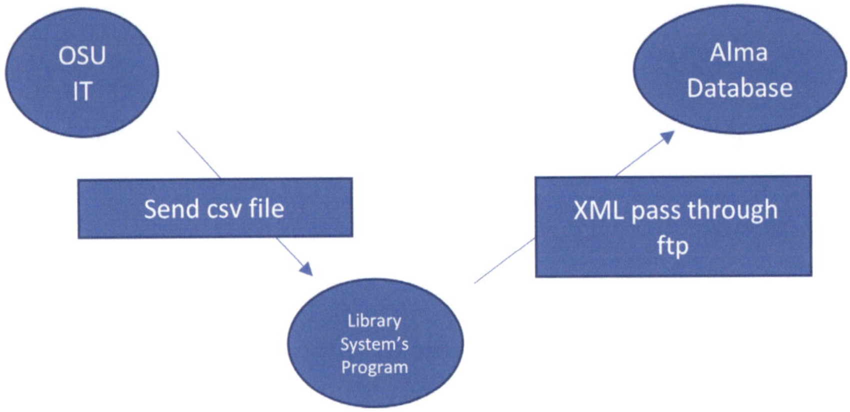

Figure 1

ways to integrate library patrons' data from the student information system. The main methods are transferring files containing the patrons' data and API integration. Currently the library uses the file transferring method, which has security and privacy issues.

As Figure 1 shows, the campus IT department sends a file containing patrons' details. The library reads those files and converts them to another format (XML). The Alma system reads those XML files and puts the patron data in the Alma database.

With this method, Library Systems can access the patrons' details, such as their full name, address, phone number, and email. Revealing those details to other people outside of campus IT and thereby increasing the number of parties who have the data may generate a security issue. Library personnel, i.e., those who are not the student information system owners, could misuse those details and even sell them to another third party.

Currently, campus IT and Library Systems use a secure channel to transfer the patrons' data files. Transferring a file with valuable data, even through a secured channel, is not adequately secure. Every day campus IT sends a file to Library Systems to maintain patrons' data. When campus IT identifies an issue with the file transfer, they manually send those files to process.

To avoid those scenarios, we can use Alma API integration as shown in Figure 2.

Campus IT uses the Alma API to push patrons' details to the Alma database. This way the library does not have to touch the patrons' details. Campus

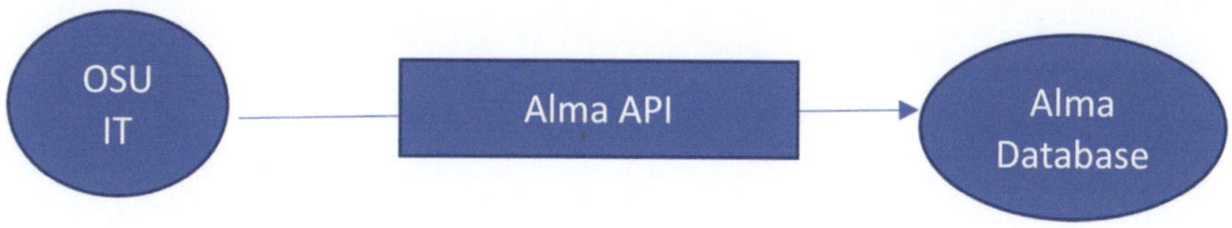

Figure 2

IT is the responsible party for the student information system owner, who has the authority to maintain and secure user details.

To access the Alma API, our approach was to use Microsoft's SQL Server Integration Services (SSIS) system. This system was able to seamlessly access the API. Also, it is capable enough to do whatever modifications are needed while transferring data. Through use of this mechanism patrons' data will not come as a file to the library and no other party can see that data.

Door Traffic Count Application

In response to COVID-19, the OSU Library developed an open-source application to better record visitor gate counts (Perera & Nykolaiszyn, 2022). This data helps inform users and administration of real-time capacity within the library's physical building. OSU Library made the decision to build the program in-house, taking advantage of cost savings and, more importantly, speed, to implement a solution quickly. After the first implementation, as an improvement, developers suggested adding cameras for each floor and to track the count of the patrons on each floor. Before implementing the process, we had several meetings to identify security and privacy concerns raised by adding cameras to the library. So, developers moved forward without implementing cameras with the application, although cameras are present in the library for general security.

CONCLUSION

The technologies developed, adopted, used, or implemented by the OSU Library in this case study represent unique and recent examples of using digital tools to solve problems and optimize library services. This has included platforms to provide instruction and educational content to students, understand user behavior on the website, develop linked open archival data, showcase faculty expertise, host open access journals, transferring data between IT and the library, server administration, and applications to improve library services such as accessing library resources and reserving study rooms. These systems create, capture, and/or are constructed entirely of grey data relating to students, researchers, instructors, staff, library users, visitors, or people documented in archival collections.

Because grey data is, by definition, *about* people, it inherently raises privacy concerns. These concerns are heightened as the systems aggregate disparate data into a single location and link it to individuals, and generate digital exhaust, or the "small data from individuals' computer-mediated actions" (Zuboff, 2015, p. 79). Furthermore, datafication, or the "rendering of social and natural worlds in machine-readable digital format" has become prevalent in multiple facets of higher education, as technologies have "enhanced the uptake and use of data for various forms of audit, inspection, evaluation and decision-making" (Williamson et al., 2020, pp. 351, 354). Datafication represents a threat to privacy inasmuch as it can influence people's professional activities and can arguably have a negative influence on their well-being (Kennedy, 2018).

The purpose of this case study has been to illustrate ways in which the OSU Library has attempted to foreground privacy considerations in administering these tools and services through dialogue, deliberation, user education, and policy development. The excitement generated by systems like learning analytics, linked open data, and RIM systems must be tempered by deliberate assessment of privacy implications, which can be slow, iterative, and based on engagement with the users and subjects. There are several other examples not explored in this paper, such as usage of and contribution to open educational resources, curation and archiving of research data, database usage statistics, and even more outside the library.

Despite the wide range of parties interested in privacy in the library, it can be difficult to develop a single, overarching policy or set of practices; however, local efforts (within departments or project teams) are still important and can have a significant impact. Indeed, institutional, state-wide, or other higher-level guidance—if any exists—is often too broad to be useful. Noting that the use of grey data "may conflict with campus privacy standards and notions of academic freedom" and that institutions often lack formal guidance, Neale and Tryniecki (2020, para. 15) recommend that universities hire Chief Privacy Officers and organize formal privacy governance boards. These initiatives can channel resources to reconcile policies across and outside the organization, conduct inventories, assess risks, define ownership, drive consensus, and build ethical technical infrastructures (Neale & Tryniecki, 2020). Given their "vocational imperative" to think critically about privacy issues, librarians should have a seat at the table in procurement and system administration decisions, and may consider offering, as a formal service, privacy assessment of any university system collecting grey data.

REFERENCES

American Library Association. (n.d.). *Privacy field guides.* The Institute of Museum and Library Services and the American Library Association. https://www.ala.org/advocacy/privacy/fieldguides

American Library Association. (2019a). *Library bill of rights.* https://www.ala.org/advocacy/intfreedom/librarybill

American Library Association. (2019b). *Privacy: An interpretation of the library bill of rights.* https://www.ala.org/advocacy/intfreedom/librarybill/interpretations/privacy

American Library Association. (2021a). *Code of ethics.* https://www.ala.org/tools/ethics

American Library Association. (2021b). *Privacy.* https://www.ala.org/advocacy/privacy

American Library Association. (2021c). *State privacy laws regarding library records.* https://www.ala.org/advocacy/privacy/statelaws

Asher, A. D., Briney, K., A., Jones, K. L. M., Regalado, M., Perry, M. R., Goben, A., Smale, M. A., & Salo, D. (2022). Questions of trust: A survey of student expectations and perspectives on library learning analytics. *The Library Quarterly, 92*(2), 151–171. https://doi.org/10.1086/718605

Asher, A., Briney, K., Gardner, G., Hinchliffe, L., Levernier, J., Nowviskie, B., Salo, D., & Shorish, Y. (2018). *Ethics in research use of library patron data: Glossary and explainer.* Digital Library Federation: Technologies of Surveillance Group. https://doi.org/10.17605/OSF.IO/XFKZ6

Aspesi, C. (2019). *SPARC landscape analysis.* Scholarly Publishing and Academic Resources Coalition. https://doi.org/10.31229/osf.io/58yhb

Auraria Library. (2020). *Auraria Library privacy statement.* https://library.auraria.edu/about/privacy-statement

Balkin, J. M. (2016). Information fiduciaries and the First Amendment. *UC Davis Law Review, 49*(4), 1183–1234. https://lawreview.law.ucdavis.edu/issues/49/4/Lecture/49-4_Balkin.pdf

Bettinger, E., Burnett, M., Gibeault, M., Shorish, Y., & Walker, P. (2019). *Advocacy action plan.* Digital Library Federation: Technologies of Surveillance Group. https://doi.org/10.17605/OSF.IO/J5K8S

Borgman, C. L. (2018). Open data, grey data, and stewardship: Universities at the privacy frontier. *Berkeley Technology Law Journal, 33*(2), 365–412. https://www.jstor.org/stable/26533142 (https://doi.org/10.15779/Z38B56D489)

Briney, K. A. (2019). Data management practices in academic library learning analytics: A critical review. *Journal of Librarianship and Scholarly Communication, 7*(1), 1–39. https://doi.org/10.7710/2162-3309.2268

Briney, K., Yoose, B., Ockerbloom, J. M., & Swauger, S. (2020). *A practical guide to performing a library user data risk assessment in library-built systems.* Digital Library Federation: Privacy and Ethics in Technology Working Group. http://doi.org/10.17605/OSF.IO/V2C3M

Bryant, R., Clements, A., de Castro, P., Cantrell, J., Dortmund, A., Fransen, J., Gallagher, P., & Mennielli, M. (2018). *Practices and patterns in research information management: Findings from a global survey.* OCLC Research. https://doi.org/10.25333/BGFG-D241

Bryant, R., Fransen, J., de Castro, P., Helmstutler, B., & Scherer, D. (2021a). *Research information management in the United States: Part 1—findings and recommendations.* OCLC Research. https://doi.org/10.25333/8hgy-s428

Bryant, R., Fransen, J., de Castro, P., Helmstutler, B., & Scherer, D. (2021b). *Research information management in the United States: Part 2—case studies.* OCLC Research. https://doi.org/10.25333/qv1f-9e57

Caines, A. (n.d.). *Technoethics DigCiz.* https://technoethics.digciz.org/

Chisholm, A., & Hartman-Caverly, S. (2018). *Privacy workshop* [Lesson plan]. ACRL Framework for Information Literacy Sandbox. https://sandbox.acrl.org/library-collection/privacy-workshop

Chisholm, A., & Hartman-Caverly, S. (2021). *Privacy workshop* [Lesson plan]. ACRL Framework for Information Literacy Sandbox. https://sandbox.acrl.org/library-collection/privacy-workshop-peerprofessional

Chisholm, A., & Hartman-Caverly, S. (2022). *Digital shred privacy literacy toolkit.* https://sites.psu.edu/digitalshred/category/teaching-materials/

Collier, A. (2017). Digital sanctuary: Protection and refuge on the web? *EDUCAUSEreview, September/October 2017*, 56–57. https://er.educause.edu/articles/2017/8/digital-sanctuary-protection-and-refuge-on-the-web

Colquhoun, C., Essmiller, K., & Reiter, H. (2021, April 13–16). *Col Mustard in the library with learning analytics: The student data privacy game* [Conference session]. 2021 Association of College and Research Libraries conference. https://hdl.handle.net/11244/335517

Cooper, D. (2021). *Views from library leadership.* Licensing Privacy Project. https://publish.illinois.edu/licensingprivacy/white-papers/

Doty, P. (2020). Library analytics as moral dilemmas for academic librarians. *The Journal of Academic Librarianship, 46*(4), 1–5. https://doi.org/10.1016/j.acalib.2020.102141

Drachsler, H., & Greller, W. (2016). *Privacy and analytics — it's a DELICATE issue: A checklist for trusted learning analytics.* Proceedings of the Sixth International Conference on Learning Analytics & Knowledge, 89–98. https://doi.org/10.1145/2883851.2883893

Electronic Frontier Foundation. (n.d.). *Tools from EFF's tech team.* https://www.eff.org/pages/tools

Family Educational Rights and Privacy, 34 C.F.R. § 99.31. (2011). https://studentprivacy.ed.gov/node/548/#0.1_se34.1.99_131

Federal Trade Commission. (2021). *How to protect your privacy on apps.* Federal Trade Commission Consumer Advice. http://consumer.ftc.gov/articles/how-protect-your-privacy-apps

Feinstein, E., Frank, E., Gabler, V., Hall, R., Holland, C., Langham-Putrow, A., Minor, D., Roh, C., & Swift, A. (2018). *Scholarly communications infrastructure checklist.* https://doi.org/10.6084/m9.figshare.7406849

Google. (2023). *Google Analytics Opt-out Browser Add-on.* https://tools.google.com/dlpage/gaoptout

Hanson, C. (2019, April 8–9). *User tracking on academic publisher platforms* [Keynote]. EResources MN Conference 2019. https://www.codyh.com/writing/tracking.html

Hartman-Caverly, S., & Chisholm, A. (2020). Privacy literacy instruction practices in academic libraries: Past, present, and possibilities. *Information Federation of Library Associations and Institutions, 46*(4), 305–327. https://doi.org/10.1177/0340035220956804

Hartman-Caverly, S., & Chisholm, A. (2021a). *Intellectual privacy workshop* [Lesson plan]. ACRL Framework for Information Literacy Sandbox. https://sandbox.acrl.org/library-collection/intellectual-privacy-workshop-peerprofessional

Hartman-Caverly, S., & Chisholm, A. (2021b). *Privacy and dx workshop* [Lesson plan]. ACRL Framework for Information Literacy Sandbox. https://sandbox.acrl.org/library-collection/privacy-and-dx-digital-transformation-workshop-peerprofessional

Heller, M., & Galvan, S. (2020). *Vendor privacy policy analysis project.* The Digital Library Federation's Privacy and Ethics in Technology Working Group. https://osf.io/69svz/

Hinchliffe, L. J. (n.d.). *The project.* Licensing Privacy. https://publish.illinois.edu/licensingprivacy/

Hinchliffe, L. J., & Jones, K. M. L. (n.d.). *Prioritizing privacy.* https://prioritizingprivacy.org/

Indiana University Libraries. (2012). *Indiana University Libraries privacy policy.* https://policies.iu.edu/policies/lib-01-libraries-privacy/index.html#policyStatement

Intellectual Freedom Committee. (2020). *Library privacy guidelines for vendors.* American Library Association. https://www.ala.org/advocacy/privacy/guidelines/vendors

International Learning Analytics and Knowledge Conference. (2010, July 22). *Learning analytics & knowledge: February 27–March 1, 2011.* https://tekri.athabascau.ca/analytics/

Irvin, D. (2021). Ethics, encryption, and evolving concepts of personal privacy in the "black box library." *The Serials Librarian, 81*(1), 35–41. https://doi.org/10.1080/0361526X.2021.1875960

Jones, K. M. L. (2019). "Just because you can doesn't mean you should": Practitioner perceptions of learning analytics ethics. *Libraries and the Academy, 19*(3), 407–428. https://doi.org/10.1353/pla.2019.0025

Jones, K. M. L., Asher, A., Goben, A., Perry, M. R., Salo, D., Briney, K. A., & Robertshaw, M. B. (2020). "We're being tracked at all times": Student perspectives of their privacy in relation to learning analytics in higher education. *Journal of the Association for Information Science and Technology, 71*(9), 1044–1059. https://doi.org/10.1002/asi.24358

Jones, K. M. L., Briney, K. A., Goben, A., Salo, D., Asher, A., & Perry, M. R. (2020). A comprehensive primer to library learning analytics practices, initiatives, and privacy issues. *College & Research Libraries, 81*(3), 570–591. https://doi.org/10.5860/crl.81.3.570

Jones, K. M. L., Perry, M. R., Goben, A., Asher, A., Briney, K. A., Robertshaw, M. B., & Salo, D. (2019). *In their own words: Student perspectives on privacy and library participation in learning analytics initiatives.* Proceedings from the 2019 ACRL Conference. https://osf.io/nfqv8/

Jones, K. M. L., Rubel, A., & LeClere, E. (2020). A matter of trust: Higher education institutions as information fiduciaries in an age of educational data mining and learning analytics. *Journal of the Association for Information Science and Technology, 71*(10), 1227–1241. https://doi.org/10.1002/asi.24327

Jones, K. M. L., & Salo, D. (2018). Learning analytics and the academic library: Professional ethics commitments at a crossroads. *College & Research Libraries, 79*(3), 304–323. https://doi.org/10.5860/crl.79.3.304

Jones, K. M. L., VanScoy, A., Bright, K., Harding, A., & Vedak, S. (2022). A measurement of faculty views on the meaning and value of student privacy. *Journal of Computing in Higher Education, 34*(3), 769–789. https://doi.org/10.1007/s12528-022-09320-7

Kennedy, H. (2018). Living with data: Aligning data studies and data activism through a focus on everyday experiences of datafication. *Krisis: Journal for Contemporary Philosophy, 2018*(1), 18–30. http://eprints.whiterose.ac.uk/129959/

Kumar, P. C., & Byrne, V. L. (2022). The 5Ds of privacy literacy: A framework for privacy education. *Information and Learning Sciences, 123*(7/8), 445–461. https://doi.org/10.1108/ILS-02-2022-0022

Kurzweil, M., & Stevens, M. (2018). Setting the table: Responsible use of student data in higher education. *Educause Review, May/June 2018*, 17–24. https://er.educause.edu/articles/2018/5/setting-the-table-responsible-use-of-student-data-in-higher-education

LDH Consulting Services. (2022). *Developing the vendor contract and policy rubric.* Licensing Privacy Project. https://publish.illinois.edu/licensingprivacy/white-papers/

Lentzsch, C., Shah, S. J., Andow, B., Degeling, M., Das, A., & Enck, W. (2021, February 21–25). *Hey Alexa, is this skill safe?: Taking a closer look at the Alexa skill ecosystem* [Paper presentation]. Network and Distributed Systems Security (NDSS) Symposium 2021. https://doi.org/10.14722/ndss.2021.23111

Lewis, T., Gangadharan, S. P., Saba, M., & Petty, T. (2018). *Digital defense playbook: Community power tools for reclaiming data.* Our Data Bodies. https://www.odbproject.org/tools/

Li, W., Sun, K., Schaub, F., & Brooks, C. (2021). Disparities in students' propensity to consent to learning analytics. *International Journal of Artificial Intelligence in Education, 32*, 564–608. https://doi.org/10.1007/s40593-021-00254-2

Library Freedom. (n.d.). *Crash courses.* https://libraryfreedom.org/crashcourse/

Lively, T. K. (2022). *Connecticut enacts comprehensive consumer data privacy law.* International Association of Privacy Professionals (IAPP). https://iapp.org/news/a/connecticut-enacts-comprehensive-consumer-data-privacy-law/

Luzeckyj, A., West, D. S., Searle, B. K., Toohey, D. P., Vanderlelie, J. J., & Bell, K. R. (2020). Stakeholder perspectives (staff and students) on institution-wide use of learning analytics to improve learning and teaching outcomes. In D. Ifenthaler & D. Gibson (Eds.), *Adoption of data analytics in higher education learning and teaching* (pp. 177–200). Springer. https://doi.org/10.1007/978-3-030-47392-1_10

Macken, M., Chartier, M., Milligan, S., & Pearson-Little Thunder, J. (2023). The Oklahoma native artists project: Oral histories to linked open data. In A. Provo, K. Burlingame, & B. M. Watson (Eds.), *Ethics in linked data.* Litwin Books & Library Juice Press.

Macken, M., & Iakovakis, C. (2021). Privacy and research information management systems. *The Serials Librarian, 81*(1), 88–98. https://doi.org/10.1080/0361526X.2021.1875959

McKinnon, D., & Turp, C. (2022). Are library vendors doing enough to protect users? A content analysis of major ILS privacy policies. *The Journal of Academic Librarianship, 48*(2), 1–8. https://doi.org/10.1016/j.acalib.2022.102505

National Information Standards Organization. (2015). *NISO consensus principles on user's digital privacy in library, publisher, and software-provider systems.* https://www.niso.org/publications/privacy-principles

Neale, M., & Tryniecki, M. (2020). *Shades of grey: The evolution of data privacy standards in higher education.* EDUCAUSE Review: Industry Insights. https://er.educause.edu/blogs/sponsored/2020/2/shades-of-grey-the-evolution-of-data-privacy-standards-in-higher-education

Nelson, A. (2022). Ensuring free, immediate, and equitable access to federally funded research. https://www.whitehouse.gov/wp-content/uploads/2022/08/08-2022-OSTP-Public-Access-Memo.pdf

Nichols Hess, A., LaPorte-Fiori, R., & Engwall, K. (2015). Preserving patron privacy in the 21st century academic library. *The Journal of Academic Librarianship, 41*(1), 105–114. https://doi.org/10.1016/j.acalib.2014.10.010

O'Brien, P., W.H. Young, S., Arlitsch, K., & Benedict, K. (2018). Protecting privacy on the web: A study of HTTPS and Google Analytics implementation in academic library websites. *Online Information Review, 42*(6), 734–751. https://doi.org/10.1108/OIR-02-2018-0056

Oakleaf, M. (2010). *The value of academic libraries: A comprehensive research review and report.* Association of College and Research Libraries. https://acrl.ala.org/value/?page_id=21

Oakleaf, M. (2016). Getting ready & getting started: Academic librarian involvement in institutional learning analytics initiatives. *The Journal of Academic Librarianship, 42*(4), 472–475. https://doi.org/10.1016/j.acalib.2016.05.013

Oakleaf, M., Whyte, A., Lynema, E., & Brown, M. (2017). Academic libraries & institutional learning analytics: One path to integration. *The Journal of Academic Librarianship, 43*(5), 454–461. https://doi.org/10.1016/j.acalib.2017.08.008

Oklahoma Computer Data Privacy Act, H.B. 1030, 2023 Regular Session. (2023). http://www.oklegislature.gov/BillInfo.aspx?Bill=HB1030&session=2300

Oklahoma Oral History Research Program. (2022). *Oklahoma Native Art.* Oklahoma State University. https://oknativeart.library.okstate.edu

Oklahoma State University Library Teaching & Learning. (2021). *Student data privacy guidelines.* https://info.library.okstate.edu/RLS/student-data-privacy-guidelines

Oklahoma State University. (2017). *Privacy notice.* https://go.okstate.edu/tos/privacy.html

Oklahoma State University. (2019). *Data stewardship: Data classification policy, responsibilities and guidelines* (Policy no. 3–0602). https://adminfinance.okstate.edu/policies/index.html

Oklahoma Statute 65, §65-1-105. (2013). http://www.oklegislature.gov/osStatuesTitle.aspx

Open University. (n.d.). *Student policies and regulations: Ethical use of student data for learning analytics.* https://help.open.ac.uk/documents/policies/ethical-use-of-student-data

Oral History Association. (2018). *OHA principles and best practices.* Oral History Association. https://www.oralhistory.org/principles-and-best-practices-revised-2018/

Pardo, A., & Siemens, G. (2014). Ethical and privacy principles for learning analytics. *British Journal of Educational Technology, 45*(3), 438–450. https://doi.org/10.1111/bjet.12152

Paris, B., Reynolds, R., & McGowan, C. (2021). Sins of omission: Critical informatics perspectives on privacy in e-learning systems in higher education. *Journal of the Association for Information Science and Technology, 73*(5), 708–725. https://doi.org/10.1002/asi.24575

Perera, D., & Nykolaiszyn, J. (2022). *Creating an open-source solution to record library gate counts* [Poster presentation]. SHAREOK. https://shareok.org/handle/11244/335882

Prinsloo, P., & Slade, S. (2013). *An evaluation of policy frameworks for addressing ethical considerations in learning analytics.* Proceedings of the Third International Conference on Learning Analytics and Knowledge, 240–244. https://doi.org/10.1145/2460296.2460344

Privacy Shield. (n.d.). *Privacy Shield overview.* Retrieved July 13, 2022, from https://www.privacyshield.gov/Program-Overview

Public Knowledge Project. (2018). *GDPR guidebook for PKP users.* PKP Docs. https://docs.pkp.sfu.ca/gdpr/en/

Research Data Alliance International Indigenous Data Sovereignty Interest Group. (2019). CARE principles for Indigenous data governance. *The Global Indigenous Data Alliance.* https://www.gida-global.org/care

Rhoades, A. (2020). Big tech makes big data out of your child: The FERPA loophole edtech exploits to monetize student data. *American University Business Law Review, 9*(3), 445–474.

Roberts, L. D., Chang, V., & Gibson, D. (2017). Ethical considerations in adopting a university- and system-wide approach to data and learning analytics. In B. Kei Daniel (Ed.), *Big data and learning analytics in higher education* (pp. 89–108). Springer International Publishing. https://doi.org/10.1007/978-3-319-06520-5_7

Rotman, D. (2009, February 8–11). *Are you looking at me? - Social media and privacy literacy* [Poster presentation]. iConference 2009, Chapel Hill, North Carolina. https://www.ideals.illinois.edu/items/15369

Russell, N. C., Reidenberg, J. R., Martin, E., & Norton, T. B. (2018). Transparency and the marketplace for student data. *Center on Law and Information Policy, Fordham Law School.* https://ir.lawnet.fordham.edu/clip/4/

Salo. (2021). Physical-equivalent privacy. *The Serials Librarian, 81*(1), 20–34. https://doi.org/10.1080/0361526X.2021.1875962

Slade, S., Prinsloo, P., & Khalil, M. (2019). *Learning analytics at the intersections of student trust, disclosure and benefit.* Proceedings of the 9th International Conference on Learning Analytics & Knowledge, 235–244. https://doi.org/10.1145/3303772.3303796

SourceMD. (2022). In *Wikidata.* https://www.wikidata.org/wiki/Wikidata:SourceMD

Stanford Libraries. (n.d.). *Statement on patron privacy and database access.* https://library.stanford.edu/using/special-policies/statement-patron-privacy-and-database-access

Stauss, D. (2022, March 23). *Oklahoma House passes consumer data privacy bill.* Husch Blackwell. https://www.bytebacklaw.com/2022/03/oklahoma-house-passes-consumer-data-privacy-bill/

Trepte, S., Teutsch, D., Masur, P. K., Eicher, C., Fischer, M., Hennhöfer, A., & Lind, F. (2015). Do people know about privacy and data protection strategies? Towards the "online privacy literacy scale" (OPLIS). In S. Gutwirth, R. Leenes, & P. de Hert (Eds.),

Law, Governance and Technology Series: Vol. 20. Reforming European data protection law (pp. 333–365). Springer. https://doi.org/10.1007/978-94-017-9385-8_14

University of California Berkeley. (n.d.). *Learning data principles.* https://rtl.berkeley.edu/learning-data-principles

University of California San Diego. (n.d.). *Privacy 101 workshop.* https://privacy.ucsd.edu/trainings/index.html

University of California Research Information Management Systems (RIMS) Working Group. (2021). *The use of research information management systems (RIMS) at the University of California.* University of California. https://ucsf.app.box.com/s/wujuxsdsujnm3y4lu4mqj5u7kj5bq27d

University of Hawai'i at Mānoa. (2018). *Resolution supporting learning data privacy principles and practices.* Mānoa Faculty Senate. https://www.hawaii.edu/uhmfs/issues/resolution-supporting-learning-data-privacy-principles-and-practices/

University of Michigan Information and Technology Services. (n.d.). *ViziBLUE: Your library data.* Retrieved June 24, 2022, from https://safecomputing.umich.edu/viziblue/library-data

Utz, C., Amft, S., Degeling, M., Holz, T., Fahl, S., & Schaub, F. (2022). *Privacy rarely considered: Exploring considerations in the adoption of third-party services by websites* (arXiv:2203.11387). arXiv. https://doi.org/10.48550/arXiv.2203.11387

Valenti, S. J., Lund, B. D., & Beckstrom, M. A. (2022). *Library patrons' privacy: Questions and answers.* ABC-CLIO, LLC.

Vallor, S., Green, B., & Raicu, I. (2018). *Ethics in technology practice: A toolkit.* The Markkula Center for Applied Ethics at Santa Clara University. https://www.scu.edu/media/ethics-center/technology-ethics/Overview-of-Ethics-in-Tech-PracticeFinal.pdf

Value in Academic Libraries' Subcommittee on Learning Analytics and Privacy. (2021). *Learning analytics toolkit: Privacy and ethics.* Association of College and Research Libraries. Retrieved 24 June, 2022, from https://acrl.libguides.com/val/latoolkit/privacyandethics

Vaughan, J. (2020). Library privacy policies. *Library Technology Reports, 56*(6). https://doi.org/10.5860/ltr.56n6

Walker, P., Ferguson, J., Rowell, C. J., Shorish, Y., Bettinger, E., & Patterson, B. (2019). *Digital privacy instruction curriculum* [Workshop]. 2019 Digital Library Federation Forum, Tampa, FL. https://doi.org/10.17605/OSF.IO/SEBHF

WikiProject Program for Cooperative Cataloging (PCC) Wikidata Pilot. (2020). In *Wikidata.* https://www.wikidata.org/wiki/Wikidata:WikiProject_PCC_Wikidata_Pilot

Williamson, B., Bayne S., & Shay, S. (2020). The datafication of teaching in higher education: Critical issues and perspectives. *Teaching in Higher Education, 25*(4), 351–365. https://doi.org/10.1080/13562517.2020.1748811

Young, J. R. (2020). *As Instructure changes ownership, academics worry whether student data will be protected.* EdSurge. https://www.edsurge.com/news/2020-01-17-as-instructure-changes-ownership-academics-worry-whether-student-data-will-be-protected

Young, S. W. H., Clark, J. A., Mannheimer, S., & Hinchliffe, L. J. (2019). *A national forum on web privacy and web analytics: Action handbook.* A National Forum on Web Privacy and Web Analytics. https://doi.org/10.15788/20190416.15446

Zeide, E. (2016). Student privacy principles for the age of Big Data: Moving beyond FERPA and FIPPS. *Drexel Law Review, 8*(2), 339–394.

Zeide, E. (2017). The limits of education purpose limitations. *University of Miami Law Review, 71*(2), 494–527. https://repository.law.miami.edu/umlr/vol71/iss2/8

Zoss, A., Gatlin, S., Girardeau, A., Guthrie, B., Healy, C., Hill, J., Wickes, A., & McGeary, T. (2021). *Priorities and guiding principles for protecting patron privacy*. Duke University Libraries' Data Privacy and Retention Task Force. https://hdl.handle.net/10161/23594

Zuboff, S. (2015). Big other: Surveillance capitalism and the prospects of an information civilization. *Journal of Information Technology, 30*(1), 75–89. https://doi.org/10.1057/jit.2015.5

LIBRARY DATA PRIVACY POLICY
Insights From Existing Policies

Brady Lund

This chapter explores library data privacy policies: policies that guide how data may be collected and used by a library and its website. These policies are important pieces of information for patrons. They communicate to patrons whether your library can be trusted to uphold the professional values of privacy and intellectual freedom, or if patrons must be additionally cautious about what information they access within the library and on library websites (Hess et al., 2015). Certainly, with the number of challenges to library materials and invasions to the privacy of citizens reaching unparalleled levels in recent years, libraries want to provide as much comfort to patrons as possible. However, there are also compelling reasons to collect data to improve library services and demonstrate the library's value to its community. The need to balance the collection of data for library improvement purposes with the patron's right to privacy is difficult and necessitates a carefully crafted policy that can serve as a framework for practice. In this chapter, we will look at the basis and necessity of privacy policy, current policy practices in public and academic libraries, and how a library can go about creating a new privacy policy from scratch.

WHAT IS A DATA PRIVACY POLICY? WHY SHOULD LIBRARIES HAVE ONE?

The purpose of a data privacy policy is to codify the processes by which patron data (data collected about the patron by the library and its systems) may be collected, stored, and used by libraries and to communicate these processes to the patrons themselves so that they can make informed decisions about their library use. As with any policy, a data privacy policy is likely to be most effective when it educates the reader about relevant risks in addition to informing the reader what the organization does to handle this data and protect users. Consider that data is a broad, ambiguous, and distant concept for many people. Many patrons may lack an understanding of what data exists about them and how systems store this data. They may be shocked to find that personal information about them already exists on the web, through sites like the Whitepages and Mylife, where addresses, phone numbers, and, in many cases, data like ethnicity, age, and income, are publicly available. Several recent studies suggest that only about one-third of the general public truly understand the extent to which their data is collected, stored, and shared online (Kennedy et al., 2021; Nidup, 2021; Sichel, 2021). A data privacy policy can be an opportunity to educate about data privacy in general, in addition to library data privacy specifically.

Ambiguity or the use of jargon in privacy policies can be problematic, as it can leave the reader with enhanced concern about privacy risks rather than trust in the organization's ability to secure the data (Pollach, 2007). The length and wordiness of a policy can also present issues, as readers may be unwilling to read the policy and, as a result, lack an understanding of their privacy rights and risks (McDonald & Cranor, 2008). Thus, it is important that these policies, while comprehensive, are also succinct. The average attention span of web users is less than one minute (Jampp, 2016). This means that the optimal policy should likely be no more than 300 words in length (most guides suggest that adults read at a rate of about 200–300 words per minute), though by using elements like bullet points and short paragraphs to break up sections of text, it may be extended.

Different types of libraries will undoubtedly have different needs as to what content is included in a data privacy policy. Larger libraries may be actively involved in collecting certain web usage data about their patrons in order to improve services, while a small, rural library may collect hardly any data at all, and thus be mainly focused on how external sites and browsers collect data about their patrons. Depending on the size of the library/library system and any parent organization (such as the university system in the case of an academic library), there may be certain elements of the policy that are dictated from higher up in the organization and cannot be contradicted. If university administrations dictate that data related to use of campus resources will be collected, then the academic library cannot really avoid that edict. However, all libraries should do everything within their means to create the most air-tight and easy-to-understand policy possible for their patrons. Adherence to this policy is crucial to ensure patrons' rights and safeguard their interests.

As it is often wise to engage in evidence-based practice—using existing work to inform library practice—the following sections describe the findings of two studies of public and academic library data privacy policies. These studies highlight the current policy practices of these libraries and suggest what an effective policy might look like. These findings will then inform the discussion in the closing sections of the chapter.

PUBLIC LIBRARY DATA PRIVACY POLICIES

This section about public library privacy policies is based in part on the findings of a study which originally appeared in the academic journal *Serials Librarian* (Lund, 2021). However, the writing in this chapter is all original and incorporates several new analyses of the data.

For the study of public libraries, a random sample of 1000 public libraries (representing a range of library sizes, service populations, and geographies) was selected from the list of public libraries compiled by the Institute of Museum and Library Services. After the list of 1000 libraries was compiled, the researcher visited the website of each library to determine whether a data privacy policy was publicly available on the library's website (if the library had multiple branches, the main branch was used). If no policy was found on the website, the library was contacted in an attempt to determine whether a policy existed in any form. The content of all policies was transferred to Microsoft Excel and then RapidMiner (a data mining software) for further analysis. Of the public library websites studied, 446 (44.6%) had a privacy policy available. The following subsections explore what factors tend to predict the presence/absence of a policy as well as what the content of different policies tell us about how data privacy is currently viewed among public libraries.

INDICATORS OF THE EXISTENCE OF A PUBLIC LIBRARY DATA PRIVACY POLICY

The findings of a prior study of public libraries presented preliminary insights into data privacy policies. When analyzed using correlation analysis, no statistically significant relationship was found between the existence of a public library privacy policy and any of the six variables examined: size of library service population (correlation of .098, not statistically significant), number of annual visits (.104), number of MLS-credentialed librarians (.118), number of library branches (.151), total library income/funding (.177), or number of Wi-Fi sessions (.029). A regression analysis similarly found that none of these variables were statistically significant contributors to the existence of a library privacy policy. As will be shown in the academic library section, the absence of any correlations for public libraries differs substantially from academic libraries, where several significant relationships/predictors exist.

CONTENT OF THE DATA PRIVACY POLICIES

Table 1 displays the number of public libraries that fell into each of the five clusters. Only 446 of the 1000 library websites examined had a library privacy policy listed. Many of those libraries that did have a policy had one that many readers would likely consider ineffective, such as those that essentially said, "library users should have no expectation of privacy." While that might be true, a more effective policy could explain why that is the case. There is an opportunity to educate patrons about specific online risks so that they may at least take steps to avoid sharing as much data as possible.

Many other libraries took the approach of pointing to legislation or the Library Bill of Rights (LBOR) as a source for their own library privacy policy. This is probably the "easiest" approach, as it shifts some blame for any issues with the policy to these original sources. Of these two sources for policy, the LBOR is probably the most meaningful, as it is a set of principles designed specifically for libraries, whereas legislation tends to be more general (policy that is written for and applies to many industries where private citizens' data is collected, not just libraries).

Table 1. Clusters and frequencies for public library data privacy policies.

Cluster	**1**	**2**	**3**	**4**	**5**
Number of Libraries in Cluster	63	89	63	121	110
"Name"	"No Expectation of Privacy"	Computers are not secure; however, we do our best to ensure our community's security	We will follow law and enforce procedure	We will uphold the Library Bill of Rights	Computer Privacy Detailed
Description	Libraries that inform patrons that, with the internet, there should be no expectation of privacy at any times (so be risk aware!)	Libraries that inform patrons that there should be no expectation of privacy; however, the library will do what it can on its part to support security (by regularly educating the public and purging any data held within the library)	Libraries that reference federal, state, or local law as the basis for privacy procedures within the library	Libraries that reference the Library Bill of Rights and/or professional ethics of librarianship as the basis for privacy procedures within the library	Libraries that have seemingly more advanced privacy policies that define terminology and detail procedures (e.g., "the library regularly destroys all data archived by the computer systems")

Generally, the most effective policy for public libraries is a comprehensive privacy policy. This type of privacy policy is specifically tailored for the library and clearly outlines the various types of data that may be collected from users, the measures taken by the library to minimize risks, and the steps patrons can take to enhance their privacy.

ACADEMIC LIBRARY DATA PRIVACY POLICIES

The methods previously used to analyze public libraries were replicated in a new study of academic library data privacy policies. Based on a database of all higher education institutions in the United States provided by the National Center for Educational Statistics, 1000 higher education institutions were randomly selected for analysis. This sample represented a variety of institutional categories: research status (non-research, research university), private/public, Carnegie classification (number of students/university size). Data privacy policies were collected by visiting the website of each university and its academic libraries. This analysis looked only for publicly available policies, listed on the university's webpage, rather than contacting each library to ask if they have a policy that just may not be posted on their site. Public accessibility of data privacy policies is important, and any library that has a policy that is not posted on their site should do so immediately.

Of the academic library websites that were examined, 29.7% had a library-specific privacy policy posted. An additional 64.6% of colleges/universities had a university-wide policy listed but no library-specific policy. This means that 94.3% of academic libraries had some form of privacy policy listed either on their webpage or on their parent site's pages, while 5.7% lacked any type of privacy policy on their website.

INDICATORS OF THE EXISTENCE OF AN ACADEMIC LIBRARY DATA PRIVACY POLICY

The variables of research category (non-research = 0, research = 1), private/public college/university (private = 0, public = 1), number of students, and existence of a library privacy policy (no = 0, yes = 1) were analyzed using correlation and regression analysis to see whether any relationship exists among them. Each of the first three variables were found to positively correlate with the existence of a policy. Category correlated at a .507 level (moderately strong, positive correlation), private/public correlated at a .138 level (weak, positive), and number of students at a .386 level (moderate, positive). Number of students correlated with research category at .535 and with private/public status at .397; however, no significant correlation was found between research category and private/public status, at only .020.

The regression analysis showed that the three variables of research category, private/public status, and number of students were a fairly strong predictor of whether an academic library has a privacy policy; $r^2 = .28$, $F = 62.99$, $p < .001$. The standardized coefficients (which show the relative influence of each variable) were .443 ($p < .001$) for research category, .083 ($p = .057$) for private/public status, and .116 ($p = .024$) for number of students. These statistics indicate that public, research universities with larger numbers of students are more likely to have a specific library privacy policy available.

Lastly, the prior two analyses were reperformed for all library-specific policies, with the variable of policy length (in number of words) replacing the existence of a policy variable. The purpose of this analysis was to examine whether the three variables of research category, private/public status, and number of students are also predictive of the length/detail provided in policies. For the correlation analysis, only one variable, research category, was found to correlate with policy length at a statistically significant level, .209. Private/public status (–.046) and number of students (.124) were not found to correlate with policy length. The regression model was not statistically significant; $r^2 = .046$, $F = 2.32$, $p = .074$. None of the standardized coefficients were significant, though research category was close. For research category, the coefficient is .182 ($p = .064$), for private/public status, –.052 ($p = .562$), and for number of students, .048 ($p = .644$).

What do these statistics mean? Larger colleges/universities and research universities (and, especially, those universities that are both) are significantly more likely to have a library-specific privacy policy, based on the sample examined in this study. Research universities also tend to have longer privacy policies than non-research universities and colleges. These findings can be further substantiated by looking at some simple statistics for what percentage of each type of library has a policy, as is shown in Table 2. Clearly, the percentage of libraries without a library-specific privacy policy increases dramatically as the

Table 2. Demographics of academic libraries without data privacy policies.

Category	Percentage with No Library-Specific Privacy Policy	Percentage with No Identifiable Privacy Policy Campus-wide
Research 1	29%	0%
Research 2	57%	1%
Master's	80%	2%
Bachelor's	93%	12%
Associate's	87%	12%
Private	78%	6%
Public	64%	5%

research status of the university decreases, with the percentage nearly doubling with the drop from research 1 to research 2 universities. Additionally, 14% more private colleges and universities lack a policy than public colleges and universities.

Associate's (two-year) and bachelor's (four-year) colleges and universities can be particularly egregious offenders, as over one-tenth of each has no privacy policy posted anywhere on their school's website. This absence of any public policy whatsoever is virtually unheard of among research universities and even master's-level universities. It is worth noting that most of the schools with no policy campus-wide are very small. The mean number of students enrolled at these schools is 3500 and the median is 2000. It is also worth noting that the absence of a privacy policy on the school's website does not mean that no policy exists offline either. However, the lack of transparency about the policy on the website itself is concerning regardless of whether it exists offline.

CONTENT OF THE DATA PRIVACY POLICIES

Shown in Table 3 are the frequencies of academic library privacy policies falling into each of the five clusters, as was done with the public library policies. There are significant differences in what proportion of academic and public libraries fit into each cluster. 14% of public libraries have a policy that essentially states, "we cannot protect your privacy, so do not expect us to do so."

Table 3. Clusters and frequencies for academic library data privacy policies.

Cluster	**1**	**2**	**3**	**4**	**5**
Number of Libraries in Cluster	10	6	58	51	172
"Name"	"No Expectation of Privacy"	Computers are not secure; however, we do our best to ensure our community's security	We will follow law and enforce procedure	We will uphold the Library Bill of Rights	Computer Privacy Detailed
Description	Libraries that inform patrons that, with the internet, there should be no expectation of privacy at any times (so be risk aware!)	Libraries that inform patrons that there should be no expectation of privacy; however, the library will do what it can on its part to support security (by regularly educating the public and purging any data held within the library)	Libraries that reference federal, state, or local law as the basis for privacy procedures within the library	Libraries that reference the Library Bill of Rights and/or professional ethics of librarianship as the basis for privacy procedures within the library	Libraries that have seemingly more advanced privacy policies that define terminology and detail procedures (e.g., "the library regularly destroys all data archived by the computer systems")

Only 3% of academic libraries fit in this same cluster. 20% of public libraries fit in the cluster of "computers are not secure, but we will do our best," compared to just 2% of academic libraries. Roughly similar proportions of both library types fell under the "we will follow the law" cluster (14% for public, 20% for academic). 10% more public libraries fell in the "we will uphold the Library Bill of Rights" cluster (27% compared to 17%). A whopping 58% of academic libraries' policies fit in the "detailed policy" cluster. So, even though a smaller percentage of academic libraries had a privacy policy, those policies tended to have greater detail.

A potential benefit that some academic libraries have over public libraries is the presence of a dedicated IT department on campus. Many large universities require annual security literacy training, where campus employees must watch videos and answer questions about personal and organizational security measures like password protection, identifying phishing attempts, and ensuring that private data is securely stored. IT departments may also work directly with the library on technology and policy initiatives. So, the influence of this department on the campus may have a positive impact on the quality of policy. It may also partially explain why smaller colleges and universities' libraries tend to lack a policy, as the IT departments at smaller institutions are likely to have smaller budgets and less staffing for the promotion of security. Of course, libraries at smaller institutions of higher education are also more likely to have smaller budgets and staff sizes. There are simply fewer resources to dedicate to security efforts.

While some academic libraries, and many public libraries, are structurally disadvantaged when it comes to dedicating resources to technology and policy development, this does not mean that they must (or should) go without a privacy policy. Patrons at these smaller libraries are equally at risk as those at larger ones. While all the detailed content that goes into a privacy policy at an academic library like that at Stanford University may not be required, all libraries should at least have the capacity to create a basic policy that covers all the essential elements of library data privacy. The following section utilizes the findings from the studies of public and academic libraries' policies to identify these essential elements of a data privacy policy and then discusses how these elements can be incorporated into the existing policy of libraries of any size.

ESSENTIAL ELEMENTS OF A LIBRARY DATA PRIVACY POLICY

When putting together a new privacy policy for a library, it is useful to look at the common elements of existing policy at other libraries. Each policy is different, but there are some commonalities among them that point to the most important elements to include in any generic policy. On that basis, let us look at the elements that exist in almost all of the detailed privacy policies in both public and academic libraries:

- A statement that there is no way to guarantee privacy online or within the library as there are always risks.
- A statement of the types of data that are purposefully created and/or retained by the library, what the library does to reduce risk, and what patrons can do to protect themselves.
- A statement of relevant legislation.
- A link to the LBOR.

Most of these detailed policies start by acknowledging the limitations of privacy protections and library technology. The policy may begin by stating that there is no way to guarantee privacy because there are always some risks, even if those risks are relatively unlikely events like a hacking of a small public library's servers. The library may abate some fears by outlining what types of data are collected and what possible risks exist. For instance, perhaps some types of data (like the names of materials loaned by patrons) are not associated with other personally identifiable data (i.e., the library can see how often a book has been loaned, but not who specifically borrowed it). For data that carries elevated risks, it may help to identify who will have access to the data (i.e., only administrators). Regardless of the detail in the library privacy policy itself, these elements of what data is collected and who has access to it should be identified and known by all library employees (and available to patrons upon request).

Libraries should be aware of relevant privacy legislation within their state/country, in order to ensure compliance and inform patrons of their rights. Legislation in the area of privacy can vary widely from country to country and can have a significant impact on what a library privacy policy should look like. Member countries in the European Union differ in their privacy law from the United States, while both differ greatly from the law in many Asian countries. In some nations, the flow of personal information within the country may be relatively unstrained but is heavily constricted when it leaves the country. For instance, China is very restrictive of data that is collected by entities from outside the country but allows for relatively open flow of data among entities within the country (Calzada, 2022).

The LBOR was first adopted by the American Library Association in 1939 and has since been amended several times, most recently in 2019. The LBOR provides an ethical framework by which libraries should construct their policies. By acknowledging the LBOR, libraries strengthen their policy positions and provide a barrier against policy challenges (i.e., one can point to the LBOR when justifying the policy rather than having appearances that it was "just made up"). Regarding information and data privacy, the seventh principle in the LBOR states,

> All people, regardless of origin, age, background, or views, possess a right to privacy and confidentiality in their library use. Libraries should advocate for, educate about, and protect people's privacy, safeguarding all library use data, including personally identifiable information.
>
> (American Library Association, 2021)

AN EXAMPLE LIBRARY DATA PRIVACY POLICY

The following example of a library privacy statement and policy is based on the legislation and policy of the state of Kansas (United States). It should not be considered to be a "perfect" example, but it does incorporate most of the elements identified in the detailed data privacy policies.

Your privacy is of utmost importance to us at Shady Tree Library. We are dedicated to safeguarding your personal information and adhere to legal and professional mandates that protect your rights. Privacy is recognized as a fundamental human right in United States law since 1890 (Warren & Brandeis, 1890), and in Kansas, we strictly adhere to Chapter 45 of the State Statutes (State of Kansas, 2021), which mandates the confidentiality and security of all patron records.

Our commitment to privacy is further reinforced by the Library Bill of Rights, established by the American Library Association over eight decades ago. According to the Library Bill of Rights, all library users have the right to privacy and confidentiality in their library use, regardless of their background or views (American Library Association, 2021). We uphold this right and advocate for its protection.

Key Points:

1. Data Protection: We will never share your data with external parties without your knowledge or consent. State and federal laws prevent the sharing of data with law enforcement unless a valid search warrant is issued. In such cases, affected patrons will be promptly informed.
2. Mitigating Privacy Risks: While we cannot foresee all privacy risks, we are committed to minimizing them for our patrons. Our staff strictly maintains patron confidentiality. However, patrons are encouraged to remain vigilant in safeguarding their online privacy.
3. Types of Collected Data: To improve services and allocate resources effectively, we collect certain data, including:
    - Data for patron accounts (name, address, email address, phone number).
    - Information about fines and holds on user accounts.
    - Records of checked-out materials (deleted once per month).
    - Browsing history and search queries (without personal identifying information).
    - IP address and browser type when accessing the library website on personal devices.
    - Cookies to enhance usability and save preferences.
    - Email address and query when using the library chat service.
    - Survey data for service improvement.
    - Public records requests may affect certain communications sent using library computers.
4. Security Measures: We employ robust security measures to protect patron data, including password-protected networks and dual-factor authentication. However, complete elimination of all risks is not guaranteed.

For any concerns about data security, please contact our library systems manager, Joe Steves, at jsteves@library.org or reach out directly to the Dean of the Libraries at janders@library.org.

Your privacy is a top priority for us, and we are dedicated to providing a safe and secure environment for all patrons at Shady Tree Library.

American Library Association. (2021, October 22). *Library Bill of Rights.* Retrieved from https://ala.org/advocacy/intfreedom/librarybill/

State of Kansas. (2021, September 21). Chapter 45 – Public records, documents and information. Retrieved from https://www.ksrevisor.org/statutes/ksa_ch45.html

CONCLUSION

An effective library data privacy policy should both educate readers and serve as a framework for how data is handled within the organization. This chapter has demonstrated that many libraries—both public and academic—lack an adequate privacy policy, leaving their patrons susceptible to privacy breaches and woefully uninformed about their rights and risks. Also illustrated in this chapter are the essential elements of a library data privacy policy and how they fit together, including a statement of risks, a statement of the library's data usage and measures to mitigate risks, a statement of relevant legislation, and a reference to the Library Bill of Rights. Any public or academic library that currently lacks a privacy policy can utilize this structure to compose one.

REFERENCES

American Library Association. (2021, October 22). *Library Bill of Rights.* https://ala.org/advocacy/intfreedom/librarybill/

Calzada, I. (2022). Citizens' data privacy in China: The state of the art of the Personal Information Protection Law (PIPL). *Smart Cities, 5*(3), 1129–1150.

Hess, A. N., LaPorte-Fiori, R., & Engwall, K. (2015). Preserving patron privacy in the 21st century academic library. *The Journal of Academic Librarianship, 41*(1), 105–114.

Jampp. (2016, July 28). Consumer behavior on e-commerce mobile apps. https://www.jampp.com

Kennedy, H., Oman, S., Taylor, M., Bates, J., & Steedman, R. (2021). *Public understanding and perceptions of data practices: A review of existing research.* http://livingwithdata.org/current-research/publications/

Lund, B. D. (2021). Public libraries' data privacy policies: A content and cluster analysis. *The Serials Librarian, 81*(1), 99–107.

McDonald, A. M., & Cranor, L. F. (2008). The cost of reading privacy policies. *Journal of Law and Policy for the Information Society, 4*(3), 543–568.

Nidup, Y. (2021). Awareness about the online security threat and ways to secure the youths. *Journal of Cyber Security, 3*(3), 133–148.

Pollach, I. (2007). What's wrong with online privacy policies? *Communications of the ACM, 50*(9), 103–108.

Sichel, G. (2021). *Public awareness of data privacy and its effects* (Honors paper). Columbus, OH: Ohio Dominican University.

Warren, Samuel; Brandeis, Louis (December 15, 1890). "The Right to Privacy." *Harvard Law Review*. IV (5): 193–220.

CHAPTER 3
PRIVACY AND SETTING UP A NEW LIBRARY MANAGEMENT SYSTEM
Alma

Emily Ray

Libraries and librarians have traditionally protected patron privacy and worked to do so in many circumstances. Now, with third-party e-resources, the challenge remains, and in some ways is more complicated as it involves systems not maintained by libraries. As an e-resource librarian, I am familiar with reading e-resource product licenses and looking to see what patron data is retained, what data could be accessed by the vendor, and where the data is stored. A library management system (LMS), the successor to Integrated Library System (ILS), differs from an e-resource product in that it's both a back-end tool used by library staff to provide services and used by patrons to access materials, print and electronic. An LMS can be involved in all aspects of a library's interactions with patrons and it has access to more patron data from the institution's enterprise system (new semester patron file updates) patron identification data, circulation data, and patron requests. Thinking of an LMS involvement with patron data can be challenging as in some ways it's so built into the library's day-to-day affairs, it can seem to library staff like furniture, not something new to investigate as due diligence before signing a license for a new e-resource product. Also, libraries don't change LMS that often, and when they do, it is a serious investment in money and time. Because of this significant but rare investment, the LMS should be examined for privacy concerns as they interact with patron data in some ways and places.

In July 2021, the university where I work, University of North Florida (UNF), migrated to a new LMS, Alma, and Primo VE as a discovery layer, both owned by Ex Libris. This migration offered a new system, a next-generation LMS designed to manage e-resources in addition to physical and digital resources. Our previous system, Aleph, predated the ubiquity of electronic formats in academic libraries. The new system can perform more functions and offers workflows that better fit our needs and can provide more data on its processes. This more advanced system can export more data elements and generate more complex reports, allowing the library to analyze its workflows and demonstrate the services and resources it provides. This increase in availability of data has many benefits, but it also provides more opportunities for exposure of patron data. A more positive way to look at this system upgrade is as an opportunity to review and reconsider privacy issues and settings. In keeping an eye on privacy while migrating to a new LMS, I learned what areas of Alma to focus on for privacy, what anonymization is possible where, and I gained a better understanding of the complexity of Alma's system and configuration. I came away with a list of recommendations for our institution.

UNF has 15,400 full-time equivalents (FTEs) and is predominantly an undergraduate institution with some graduate and doctoral programs. We are a state university in Florida and a member of the State University System of Florida and the Florida Virtual Library Consortium (FLVC). The decision to migrate was led by our consortium with lots of formal involvement in the decision process by the universities and college libraries. Migrating to a new system is a massive task, but it also presented the opportunity to move to a much newer, more advanced, and more user-friendly system than our previous ILS, Aleph, also an Ex Libris product. This increase in availability of data has many benefits, but it also provides more opportunities for exposure of patron data.

Another factor in privacy concerns is that, with this much more complex system, library staff aren't the only ones working in the system. As we moved forward with Alma we learned that there are settings and configurations that UNF staff don't manage, and only Ex Libris staff can edit or change. Also, the consortium we are part of, their staff also have access to the settings and the data in our LMS. There are other settings that must be consistent across the consortium, so the member institutions shouldn't change them for processes to work. Concern for privacy has been a constant in libraries, and now with e-resources and more advanced LMS, there is the patron data to be concerned over, but also the number of non-library employees who have access to the data within the more complex third-party products.

As migration approached, I decided that my priority would be to learn my own role and area in Alma as quickly as possible. In addition, I wanted to identify the different areas in Alma in which the library would be making choices that impact privacy and to encourage those more closely involved also to consider privacy in their decisions. Of course, the Alma workflows and processes I refer to in this chapter could be changed with any Alma quarterly update. Unlike earlier LMS or ILS products, there is no stable documentation for version v.2.3, with changes in v.2.4. Alma documentation is fluid. All Alma documentation is potentially changeable in the next quarterly update or tomorrow. This documentation now in 2023 and the processes they cover will, most likely, change in the future. My main goal, the identification of areas in Alma that are key to protecting patron privacy, should remain relevant for longer.

LEARNING FROM DOING

Early in our migration, I checked to see who on our staff made a change in an Alma electronic collection. I saw our UNF identifier, "N number," and saw it was my supervisor (no surprise). But I was surprised that her home address, in addition to her name and role, displayed when I clicked on the identifier. I reported this to our library systems unit and they reported it to the consortium, who sent a ticket to Ex Libris. In addition, another librarian submitted a purchase request on behalf of a faculty member, and was also surprised to see his name and address in the request and was thus concerned that his home address would be visible to the faculty member. To round it out, a different faculty member complained when his home address was visible in the letter he received regarding a request. The home address is a mandatory field for Alma users to provide.

However, it is not necessary to display when the identifier notes who completed a task in Alma. UNF could not edit this, so we submitted a ticket and Ex Libris did make the change, so the home address no longer displays. After this change, we only saw the N number identifier, the name and role, when looking to see who changed a record or ran a job in the administration portal. Later, after I completed my Alma Admin certificate and could access the configuration area of Alma, I could see that the "ContactInformationPopUp" mapping table was not managed in our network and that Ex Libris admin had switched the Home Address fields for Public and Staff to inactive in this table to stop them from being visible outside of Fulfillment.

When I saw my colleague's home address, I was already planning to investigate privacy, but hadn't started yet. All of the ILS systems I've used working in libraries had my address as a patron, but I never accidentally saw a coworker's home address. Stumbling on this impressed on me how much data Alma had and its ability to make data viewable in unanticipated locations. As it is a complex LMS system, I was surprised where and which types of users could access patron data in Alma. It also took a while to understand all the possibilities and how to evaluate them.

WHERE TO LOOK FOR PRIVACY SETTINGS, CIRCULATION/FULFILLMENT, ALMA STRUCTURE, PATRON RECORDS, REPORTS

Once I had decided that I was going to investigate privacy in Alma, I tried to identify potential risks to patron privacy. I would first look at where I thought patron data would be at risk and then investigate who can access what data.

On the Alma user home page, a navigational bar lists Acquisitions, Resources, Discovery, Admin, Analytics. At the bottom of the navigation bar is an icon for Configuration. When I click on any of these listed areas, I can see all the tasks in that area and evaluate whether patron data is involved. If I click on Configuration, I can then click on the Alma area and see what rules or setup are listed and again evaluate for potential privacy risks. On the Alma user home page I can see the links to area tasks and Configuration setups that I did not have access to with my then permissions:

(The Alma User Interface, n.d.)

After looking at the home page for Alma users, I decided to start with the area I thought would have the most potential risk for privacy: Circulation, which is called Fulfillment in Alma. In terms of how long we keep data on patrons, we followed our consortium's guideline of deleting patron checkouts one day after the loan is completed. When a patron request is completed, the patron-identifying information is also removed. The only way that data would be retained is if there is a note documenting an issue with that loan and identifying the patron. Unless something atypical like that happens, the patron data is removed.

In Fulfillment, the Circulation Desk Manager and Operator role can see the list of patrons' requests to check out items. They can see the fines/fees of a patron and can accept payment. These users can also edit a patron's information, for example, registering a new patron or a student who was not included in the patron file from the enterprise system. However, these users cannot edit the user's primary identifier or additional identifiers.

Also in Fulfillment is Transactional Anonymity, which refers to making transactions anonymous, such as loans, requests, paid fees, and fines. Anonymizing transactions is part of configuring anonymization, which is under configuring fulfillment. Fulfillment is managed at the institutional level, in our case, meaning UNF. These settings can be configured by a General Systems administrator or a Fulfillment Administrator of an institution. They are located in Configuration–Fulfillment–General–Fulfillment Jobs Configuration, then under the "Anonymize Job" section. Loan optimization rules allow you to configure rules to set up the kind of transactional anonymity that you want to set up. (If the institution is in a consortium that does InterLibrary Loan (ILL) among the members, there are some settings that need to be consistent within the consortium, but the individual institutions can change the settings. The settings involved with Transactional Anonymity settings are not the ones that need to be consistent.)

There are multiple options in the "Anonymize Job" configuration:

- "Anonymize item loans" will delete user information in a completed loan. Loans that have open fees/fines cannot be anonymized.
- "Anonymize fines and fees" will delete user information in closed fees/fines.

- "Anonymize resource sharing requests" will delete user information in completed and deleted resource sharing requests.
- For borrowing requests, the user information is deleted in completed and deleted borrowing requests.
- For lending requests, the user information is deleted in completed and deleted requests. If there is information in the borrower's configuration that is placed in notes, the information in the notes will be retained.

The "should_anonymize_requests_immediately_when_complete" parameter in "Configuring Fulfillment Jobs," when set to true, will anonymize requests immediately and is not impacted by the other "Anonymize" configurations. It is completely independent of the Transactional Anonymizations within the Fulfillment configuration. It overrides other settings (Configuring Fulfillment Jobs, n.d.).

When this job runs, the Borrower Name and Borrower ID are removed from the History tab, but the loan remains. Alma documentation provides images of the before and after of this tab.

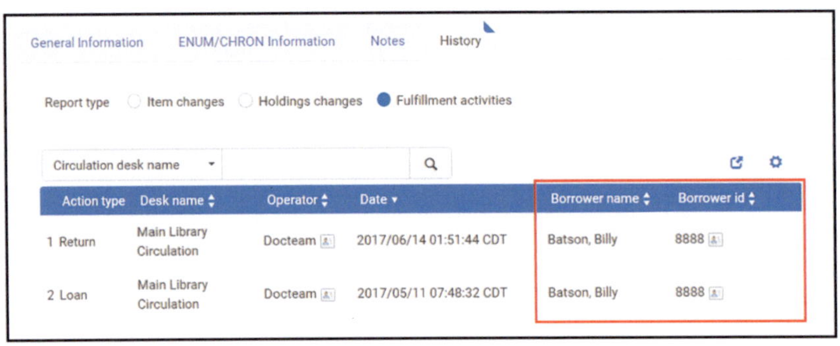

Loan History

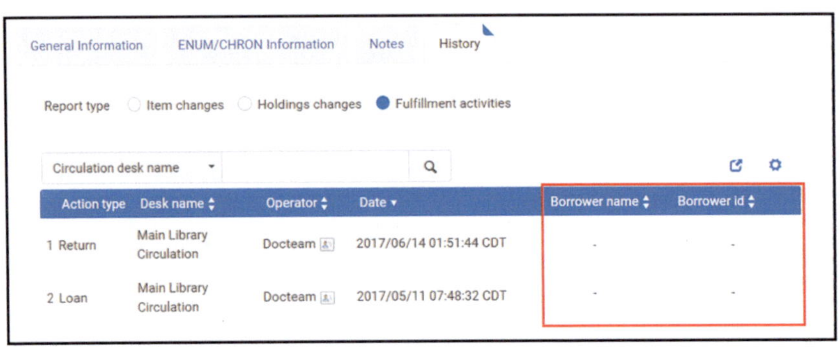

Loan History After Anonymization

Patron data is indeed present in Fulfillment. By necessity it can be seen by multiple users in Alma. There are also workflows in Fulfillment to shrink the amount of patron data kept in Alma. They work in highly specific ways and it is important to understand what task or parameter you are employing and what patron data in which specific scenarios it will hide or remove.

USER MANAGEMENT PART I

After investigating Fulfillment, I turned to User Management, which is within the Admin area. User management has the most content relating to patron data. In UNF, only the library systems unit has access to the User Management area in the Admin. At this point in the process, I was concerned by how many staff in different areas had access to these areas, for example, Fulfillment and User Management.

According to "Configuring User Groups" (Ex Libris), User Management has access to the user groups, user details, and identifiers. Only the General Systems Administrator and the User Manager, a role in User management, can edit user groups. These same two roles are the only ones who can manage the display of user names, user titles (Mr., Mrs., Ms., etc.) and user genders. Here is a screenshot of display options of user names:

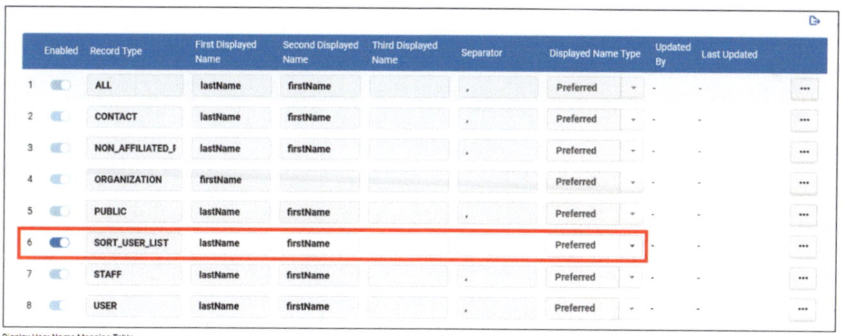

	Enabled	Record Type	First Displayed Name	Second Displayed Name	Third Displayed Name	Separator	Displayed Name Type	Updated By	Last Updated
1		ALL	lastName	firstName		,	Preferred	-	-
2		CONTACT	lastName	firstName		,	Preferred	-	-
3		NON_AFFILIATED_I	lastName	firstName		,	Preferred	-	-
4		ORGANIZATION	firstName				Preferred	-	-
5		PUBLIC	lastName	firstName		,	Preferred	-	-
6		SORT_USER_LIST	lastName	firstName			Preferred	-	-
7		STAFF	lastName	firstName		,	Preferred	-	-
8		USER	lastName	firstName		,	Preferred	-	-

Display User Name Mapping Table

User titles can be configured in the User Titles code table (Configuration–User Management–User Details–User Titles).

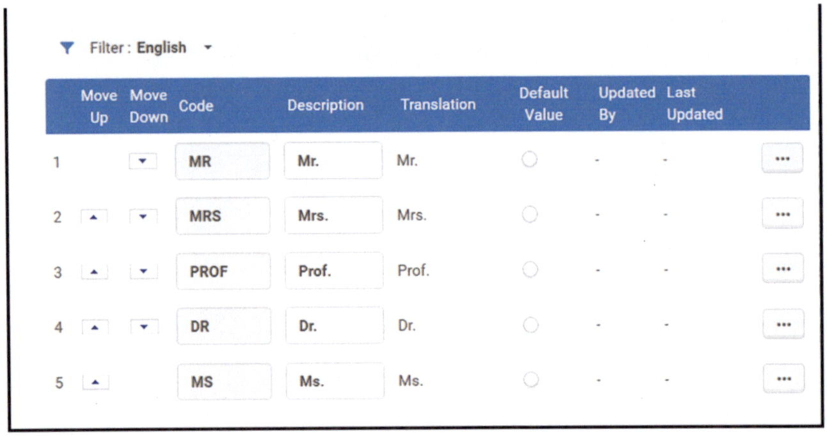

Filter : English

	Move Up	Move Down	Code	Description	Translation	Default Value	Updated By	Last Updated
1			MR	Mr.	Mr.		-	-
2			MRS	Mrs.	Mrs.		-	-
3			PROF	Prof.	Prof.		-	-
4			DR	Dr.	Dr.		-	-
5			MS	Ms.	Ms.		-	-

User Titles Code Table

Alma offers four default genders: Male, Female, None, Other. Using Additional options, up to 10 gender options are available. UNF has the four default genders as active, but in our system the gender field is greyed out and not used in our user records.

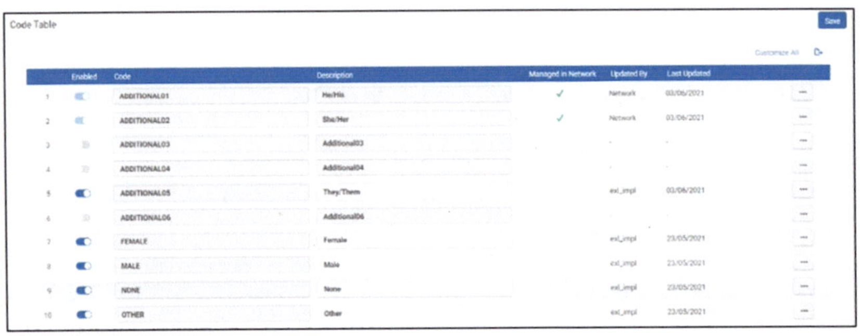

Code Table

Save

Customize All

	Enabled	Code	Description	Managed in Network	Updated By	Last Updated
1		ADDITIONAL01	He/His	✓	Network	03/06/2021
2		ADDITIONAL02	She/Her	✓	Network	03/06/2021
3		ADDITIONAL03	Additional03		-	-
4		ADDITIONAL04	Additional04		-	-
5		ADDITIONAL05	They/Them		exl_impl	03/06/2021
6		ADDITIONAL06	Additional06		-	-
7		FEMALE	Female		exl_impl	23/05/2021
8		MALE	Male		exl_impl	23/05/2021
9		NONE	None		exl_impl	23/05/2021
10		OTHER	Other		exl_impl	23/05/2021

Genders

Save

Values Notes

1 - 10 of 10 Description

Import Customize All

	Enabled	Code	Description	Managed in Network	Updated By	Last Updated
1		ADDITIONAL01	Additional01		-	-
2		ADDITIONAL02	Additional02		-	-
3		ADDITIONAL03	Additional03		-	-
4		ADDITIONAL04	Additional04		-	-
5		ADDITIONAL05	Additional05		-	-
6		ADDITIONAL06	Additional06		-	-
7		FEMALE	Female		-	-
8		MALE	Male		-	-
9		NONE	None		-	-
10		OTHER	Other		-	-

In the User Details area, two roles, User Manager and General Systems Administrator, can configure additional statistical categories from User Details for analytics reports. That includes creating the categories, defining the categories, mapping the categories, and assigning them to users for their institution. For an analytics report, five categories are the maximum. More than five categories can be created, but only up to five can be in a report. These five categories can include user group, user gender, user roles. There is potential for reports pulling together details about users that could be revealing. UNF is currently not using any of these additional categories, but we could in the future (User Details Configuration, n.d.).

Identifiers are a key data point in Alma. They connect the user's account to an outside system, such as a Student Information System, an institutional Enterprise system, or an additional fulfillment account. When the patron file is loaded at the start of a new semester, the user identifier connects that data to the user record in Alma. Every Alma (and Primo) user has a primary identifier. Institutions can enable additional user identifiers based on the user's type: public or staff. These additional user identifiers can be required or optional. Before they can be added, Ex Libris creates and configures the type of identifier. Institutions can map Alma user accounts to user accounts in external systems (for example, an external ILL system) by mapping the user identifier in Alma to the identifier in the other system. Or the institution could share their identifier with the other system.

After Ex Libris configures the types of identifiers, a User Administrator or General Systems Administrator at the institution can complete the configuration. In "Managing User Identities" they have to determine whether this additional identifier is mandatory and what default identifiers will be created when registering users (outside of the import of data from the external system). The Managing User Identities documentation states that, before creating new types of identifiers, institutions have other identifier options from outside the library: Twitter ID, Facebook ID, Google ID (as social logins); IDs relevant for Esploro (an Ex Libris product that allows researchers to create and track their work in an institutional repository); Barcode; and any other user identifier. UNF's unique identifier is our "N number," an "N" followed by an eight-digit numeral. At first I was genuinely surprised to see Twitter ID and Facebook ID as identifiers that could be used for logins. It struck me as not secure, as there are so many stories of Twitter and Facebook accounts being hacked. I posted on the Alma listserv asking for anyone whose institution, especially academic libraries, were using this and what their experience has been. No one responded to this query (Managing User Identities, n.d.).

Prior to working with Alma and Primo VE, I previously worked with EDS, the EBSCO Discovery Service. I do remember when EBSCO announced that users could now create Ebscohost accounts with Google accounts. The documentation for this is in "What is Google Sign in" in EBSCO Connect (What is Google Sign In, 2020).

The Ebscohost folder does not provide direct access to the discovery layer and all its subscription content; it's a folder where users can store articles or citations. I was not able to talk to anyone using the social logins for Alma. However, I suppose it would work with someone signing in with their Twitter or Facebook sign-in, and then the other institutional identifier in the user record triggering the authentication. A hacked social login couldn't get to anyone else's data or the institutional data as a whole, unless that user was staff with permissions. A user's hacked social login could potentially lead to illegal downloading of subscriber content.

USER MANAGEMENT PART II

Only User Manager or User Administer Roles (User Management module) can delete a user or bulk delete users. Users can be deleted when their "purge date" has passed. Users cannot be deleted if they still have outstanding fines, are currently working in the Metadata Editor, have ownership of purchase order lines or invoices, or have an active job running, etc. When a user is deleted, using "delete a user," nothing is retained and no statistical data remains for this individual user (Managing Users, n.d.).

When a bulk removal of users is done through "purging users," admins, again user management and general systems admin, can configure what data they want to retain. These are the options Alma offers.

You configure user deletion on the Delete User Policy page (**Configuration Menu > User Management > General > Delete User Policy.**

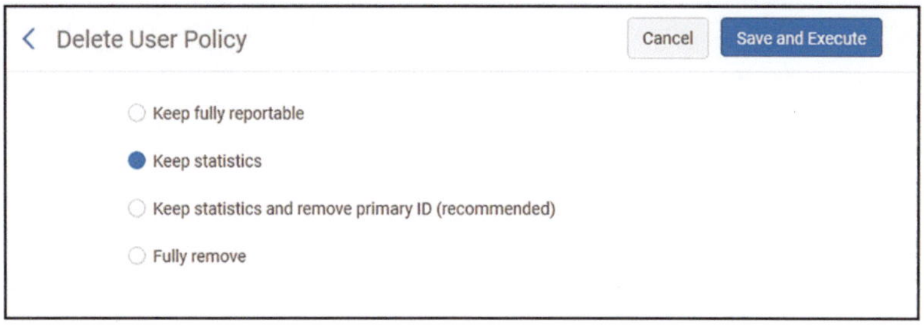

Delete User Policy Page

When an institution chooses to switch to a more restrictive option (removes more data), past data from previously purged users will be updated to that standard. I learned that UNF has the “Keep Statistics” setting selected. I plan to lobby for us to switch to “Keep statistics and remove primary ID (recommended).” I don’t believe we’d lose any of the data we wish to keep with this setting (Configuring User Deletion, n.d.).

IMPROVED ACCESS TO REPORTS IN ALMA COMPARED TO AN EARLIER, OLDER ILS: HOW TO COMPARE THE TWO?

While thinking about where more patron data was located and where it could be exposed, I asked our systems librarian what I thought at the time was a straightforward question: Do we have access to more data in Alma than we did in Aleph? If we can run more reports in Alma, then we have access to more data, and with that more reports could contain patron data, or risk violations of privacy, right? This would prove not to be so straightforward. Untangling the answer to this gave me a better understanding of the complexity of access to data in Alma.

Aleph, according to Wikipedia, was first developed to provide an LMS that could work with Hebrew and English for Israeli universities in the 1980s. By 1988, all eight existing Israeli universities used it. By 1993, the Vatican libraries used Aleph, and in 1995 200 other libraries were using it as well. Alma, again according to Wikipedia, debuted in 2011 as a cloud-based, SaaS system, labeled as an LMS (Ex Libris Group, 2022).

"We," meaning the UNF library, can run more reports with more fields, as we now have access to the analytics module in Alma. With Aleph, a set of pre-existing reports was available to all university and college library staff to run certain reports on a password-protected web interface created by the FLVC consortium. For example, I could run a report on e-resource expenditures for a fiscal year and see how much had been paid for or encumbered. My colleagues in the cataloging department could not run that report on the interface for the canned reports, as they didn't have access to the acquisition's unit in Aleph, while I could not run some cataloging reports.

Discussing this with the systems librarian, "we," UNF, can run more reports with Alma, as we can run all the reports in the Analytics unit/module. And Alma is more advanced than Aleph, so our consortium, FLVC, too, can run more reports with Alma than previously, right? My colleague wasn't sure of this. FLVC employs developers. Possibly FLVC can configure all the reports they wanted in Aleph and in Alma and there was no difference to them. I sent this as a question to our consortium: Did going from Aleph to Alma increase FLVC's access to analytics and to reports?

To quote the response I received paraphrased: "In general, there is a lot more flexibility in Alma Analytics than there was in Aleph, but there are some limitations in Alma, e.g., it's difficult to combine data from different subject areas like fulfillment and funds expenditure." Later, reading the documentation on Analytics, I think I understand why. In the documentation it stated, "In order to be able to create reports from two subject areas, there must be a common dimension between the two subject areas and the descriptive fields must come from the common dimension or dimensions" (Creating a new report, n.d.).

Structurally in Alma, Subject Areas have fact-measurement dimensions and descriptive dimensions. Facts are the factual details, for example physical measurements or monetary amounts. Dimensions are defined as "tables that contain descriptive attributes (or fields) that are typically textual fields or discrete numbers behaving like text. Dimension attributes such as Library Code, Vendor Name, or Loan Date (for example) give facts a context" (General Terminology, n.d.).

Alma also has documentation on what dimensions are shared with more than one Subject Area. For User Details, this only includes Fines and Fees, Fulfillment (called Borrower Details), Requests (called Requester), Users, Borrowing Requests (called Requester), Course Reserves (Called Librarian) (Shared Dimensions, n.d.).

My main takeaway is that the transition from Aleph to Alma is not as simple as I had earlier thought. It has more nuance and complications due to Alma's structure and internal rules. More data can be entered in the newer system, and more data can be exported or made available in reports and analytics, but it still depends on complex rules and structures and not everything is available. From attending our consortium's Analytics drop-in office hours, I see that the complexity of Alma's structure can make seemingly easy things actually be far more complex. From my limited understanding of this structure at this point, it does seem like it's not easy to combine data with User Details data that does not share a dimension with it. However, if you're satisfied with reports from only one Alma subject area, a great deal of data can be accessed from Alma analytics.

ANALYTICS

After looking at who has access to what data in Fulfillment, User Management, what identifiers our institution was using, what data can be anonymized in Fulfillment, and by whom, I moved on to the Analytics module. The Alma Analytics area is a separate module of Alma. It is listed on the main menu of the Alma User home page, but when you click on Analytics, it takes you to a different interface compared to the rest of Alma. Analytics is built on the Oracle Analytics Server and the Oracle Intelligence Business Enterprise Edition, to be more precise. Data is refreshed on a different timeline than the rest of Alma, but the Alma terminology is used in Alma Analytics. To access Alma Analytics, you need the role Design Analytics. To send reports to other users, you will need to be an Administrator of an area (Accessing Analytics, n.d.).

At first, because I had access to the Analytics module, it seemed that I could run reports from all subject areas. A colleague in our systems unit confirmed that anyone with access to the analytics module would have access to all the data in Analytics, including the User Management data in Analytics. Earlier, looking at who has access to what data in Fulfillment or User Management was not at all meaningful, as anyone who has access to Analytics can access all fields, all reports.

Early in our migration process, our library at first limited access to the Analytics module to the systems unit, but later realized that the Acquisition unit would want access to cost per use reports, reports on what order lines had been paid, etc. Also, Cataloging used reports in Alma for their annual report. All of this led to more individuals getting access to the Analytics unit in Alma.

I better see the development from Aleph by going through all the reports in the Alma documentation. Like the list of canned reports, available to us from a separate interface by our consortium for Aleph, in Alma there is also a large section of "out of the box" reports that are already configured and a user can run them as is or tweak slightly if they know how. There is also a folder of shared reports from other institutions which Alma users can copy and use locally.

In the Analytics unit and overall, I focused on where patron data could be found by someone in my position, a library employee using Alma. If I as a library employee can access the data, another library employee can, as well as staff from the company that made the product and manages it, Ex Libris. When a third-party company has access to your patrons' data, really the only real measures protecting that data are the terms in the license and the data privacy laws of the region in the license. When many library employees can access patron data, I suspect it is more likely to be used in a report to showcase what the library is doing, respecting the patrons' privacy or not. The more easily accessed the data, the more likely it is to be used? Although third-party companies can also access and use for their benefit patron data that cannot be accessed by library staff.

NON-TRANSACTIONAL ANONYMIZATION

In Fulfillment, Alma has the option of Configuring Anonymization that was applied to transactions in fulfillment. Non-transactional anonymization is covered in "Anonymizing Anonymous Report Details." If non-transactional anonymity is set up, fields such as User ID, Primary Identifier, First Name, Last Name, Middle Name, Birth Date, Job Title, Job Description, Identifier 1, Identifier 2, Note, Postal Code, Address, Preferred Contact Information,

Email, and Phone Number won't appear in reports. User Group is not a field that can be anonymized. There is another option, where all of those fields are anonymized except for First Name, Last Name, Primary Identifier. It is important to understand that the data isn't deleted from Alma; it just isn't appearing in reports. If the setting for non-transactional anonymization is removed, the data would reappear. For Alma, non-transactional anonymization is different from configuring anonymization as it doesn't relate to transactions, i.e., checkouts, requests. It isn't applied to transactions, but to the actual data. Configured anonymity occurs after the transaction has completed. Non-transactional anonymity can be applied while the actions are current or ongoing. Non-transactional anonymity can only be done by Ex Libris staff, while configuring anonymity can be done by an institution (Anonymizing Analytics Report Details, n.d.).

Considering the Analytics area it is apparent that anyone with access to Analytics can access all of the Alma reports, including Fulfillment, User Services. There are structural barriers in Alma to prevent the easy combining of data from User Services with data from other areas, but still there is a large amount of data on patrons that can be exported. Alma does provide some mechanisms in Analytics to remove patron data, but the specifics of how it works and what it removes need to be precisely understood.

ACCESS TO THE LICENSE WITH EX LIBRIS

I recently co-wrote a Library Privacy Guide for the "Vendors and Privacy" IMLS project. In the guide, I, and my co-author, Becky Yoose, suggested to other librarians looking for guidance on privacy that, if you are acquiring a resource through a consortium, ask the consortium what its privacy policies are. In addition, we recommend asking to see the license the consortium negotiated with the vendor, if you did not see the vendor's terms and conditions. For UNF, our state consortium FLVC negotiates the license and signs it with the vendor, and also pays for the product. Despite literally providing that guidance for others, I had earlier thought of the FLVC Alma license as an inaccessible document. Well into this process, I informally asked someone at the consortium if I would antagonize anyone or cause problems for myself if I asked to see the privacy section of the FLVC license with Ex Libris for Alma. This individual told me that the guidance was to file a Freedom of Information Request (FOIA request) to Florida State University (FSU). While the FLVC consortium is an independent entity, it also is hosted by one of the 12 State University System of Florida universities, and the office of general counsel reviews, signs, and stores FLVC's licenses at FSU (Vendors and Privacy, n.d.).

Florida's "Sunshine Law," in Chapter 286 of the Florida Statutes, seeks to ensure that agreements with state agencies or state organizations (including state universities) are accessible to the people of the state, and far fewer documents are deemed confidential in Florida compared to the other 49 states (Florida Legislature, n.d.). Perhaps due to this, FSU has an online form to make an FOIA request. A month before the deadline for this chapter, I requested only the section related to patron privacy in the FLVC–Ex Libris license and provided the identifying information I had related to the license. After a follow-up email, and two phone calls, I received a five-page PDF including the Customer Data section of the license and an annex covering security controls, data protection, data stewardship, and compliance. In a more perfect world, if I had submitted the FOIA request much earlier in this process, I would have followed up to request other sections potentially related to privacy. As it is, I appreciate that I was able to receive this language within a month.

In the Customer Data section, Ex Libris defines customer data as "business information, personal information or other data which a Customer and or Participating Institution stores or provides to Ex Libris for storing and processing in the SaaS Services." In this agreement, the Customer would be the consortium and UNF is one of the Participating Institutions. Ex Libris agrees during the Term "to implement reasonable security measures to protect and back up Customer Data" (this is basically meaningless) "and will at a minimum, utilize industry standard security and backup procedures." This isn't very specific, but does provide a baseline minimum of what they will do. In the Security Control section, for network security, "Ex Libris" agrees to maintain network security that—at a minimum—includes: network firewall provisioning, intrusion detection, and regular third-party penetration testing.

Likewise, "Ex Libris agrees to maintain network security that conforms to the ISO 2 700 1 standards or other generally recognized comparable standard." Also Ex Libris agrees to do a formal penetration once a year and vulnerability assessments quarterly. For security auditing, Ex Libris agrees to an "industry recognized third-party security audit that conforms to the current ISO/IEC 27001 Standard or another generally recognizable industry standard." In addition, Ex Libris has a business continuity plan and maintains cybersecurity insurance. Ex Libris also identifies the level of encryption it uses: "128 bit key AES encryption or better, including back up data."

In the Data Stewardship area, "Ex Libris acknowledges that all…Customer data…remains the sole property of the Institution…Ex Libris agrees that any and all Customer data exchanged shall be used expressly and solely for the purposes enumerated in the agreement between the Institution and Ex Libris." In regards to a legal request for Customer Data, "If required by law or a court of competent jurisdiction or an administrative body to disclose any Institution or participating academic institutional Customer Data, Ex Libris will, to the extent permitted by applicative law, notify the Institution in writing within (two) 2 days prior to any such disclosure."

At the end of the license, "Ex Libris agrees that it will handle return and deletion of Customer Data following the termination of a Subscription or the Agreement…Ex Libris will erase, destroy, or render unreadable all Institution and participating academic institutional Customer Data according to the standards enumerated in DOD 5520.22 or NIST 800–88, and upon request following completion of such erasure, certify in writing that these actions have been completed" (license between FLVC and Ex Libris, signed March 12, 2020).

In the portion of the license I have access to, Ex Libris affirms that customer data is the property of the institution, not Ex Libris. Customer data is defined and not to be shared with third parties. Ex Libris states that they will dispose of the data afterwards, confirmed in writing, if necessary. The license also specifies the security standards of its data storage and the specifications of its data security testing.

I was also looking for information about what happens to customer data if Ex Libris is purchased or acquired by another company. It is concerning that there is no language on that, especially as Ex Libris was acquired by Clarivate in December 2021. Again, I did not view the whole license, so possibly there is language on that topic in another part of the license. To be more precise,

Clarivate acquired Proquest, finalizing that deal in December 2021. Proquest owns a great deal of scholarly content and now two ILS/LMP vendors with Ex Libris and Innovative Interfaces. Clarivate on its own webpage describes itself as a research analytics company (About us, n.d.). It is commonly seen as competing with Elsevier in the market for scholarly research tools and could potentially be more interested in customer data than Ex Libris or Proquest. I have been told that our consortium's license is for six years and these terms are in effect for that time period. At this point, I don't know how or if the acquisition by Clarivate will impact customer data or patron privacy.

NEXT STEPS AND RECOMMENDATIONS

When I think about what I've learned from this process, some steps are already clear. I plan to tell colleagues that all data and all fields are available in Analytics. Permissions to Fulfillment or User Manager are not relevant; it's Analytics where the most access is located. I plan to lobby to set up transactional anonymity in Fulfillment. In some ways, we might have set up a version of that with deleting users info after the checkout or request is completed. In addition, I intend to suggest a stricter level of removing data on purged users. I think we are keeping some data on users who have purged or future purged students, and I don't see how that data would be relevant to our reports. I also plan to lobby for anonymizing data in the Analytics module. If there is pushback on these policies, I hope to have a conversation on what reports we are trying to get and if personal information about users is relevant to that.

With a fair amount of delicacy, I want to ask the consortium what levels of anonymization they are considering to use in these areas. I am hoping to get access to the section of the license covering what Ex Libris does with data if it's acquired by another company. But perhaps the real concern will be whether Clarivate will want greater access to patron data when the contract is renegotiated. In addition, this review has made clear to me how important it is to understand more about how Alma works, how this impacts what data you can get in reports, and what can be combined with patron data. It also strikes me as wise to learn more about identifiers, as there is potential for more data to be revealed with them.

REFERENCES

American Library Association. (n.d.). *Vendors and Privacy*. Retrieved July 5, 2022, from https://www.ala.org/advocacy/privacy/fieldguides

Clarivate. (n.d.). *About Us*. Clarivate. Retrieved July 5, 2022, from https://clarivate.com/#about

Ebsco. (2020, March 11). *What Is Google Sign In?* Ebsco Connect. Retrieved July 5, 2022, from https://connect.ebsco.com/s/article/Google-Sign-In-FAQS?language=en_US#:~:text=To%20sign%20into%20EBSCO%20with,are%20seamlessly%20authenticated%20into%20EBSCO

Ex Libris. (n.d.). *The Alma User Interface*. Ex Libris Knowledge Center. Retrieved July 5, 2022, from https://knowledge.exlibrisgroup.com/Alma/Product_Documentation/010Alma_Online_Help_(English)/010Getting_Started/050Alma_User_Interface_%E2%80%93_General_Information/The_Alma_User_Interface

Ex Libris. (n.d.). *Managing Patron Services*. Ex Libris Knowledge Center. Retrieved July 5, 2022, from https://knowledge.exlibrisgroup.com/Alma/Product_Documentation/010Alma_Online_Help_(English)/030Fulfillment/040Circulation_Desk_Operations/040Managing_Patron_Services

Ex Libris. (n.d.). *Configuring Fulfillment Jobs*. Ex Libris Knowledge Center. Retrieved July 5, 2022, from https://knowledge.exlibrisgroup.com/Alma/Product_Documentation/010Alma_Online_Help_(English)/030Fulfillment/080Configuring_Fulfillment/080General/Configuring_Fulfillment_Jobs#Configuring_Anonymization

Ex Libris. (n.d.). *User Details Configuration*. Ex Libris Knowledge Center. Retrieved July 5, 2022, from https://knowledge.exlibrisgroup.com/Alma/Product_Documentation/010Alma_Online_Help_(English)/050Administration/040Configuring_User_Management/040User_Details_Configuration

Ex Libris. (n.d.). *Managing User Identities*. Ex Libris Knowledge Center. Retrieved July 5, 2022, from https://knowledge.exlibrisgroup.com/Alma/Product_Documentation/010Alma_Online_Help_(English)/050Administration/030User_Management/65viewing_user_identifier_types

Ex Libris. (n.d.). *Managing Users*. Ex Libris Knowledge Center. Retrieved July 5, 2022, from https://knowledge.exlibrisgroup.com/Alma/Product_Documentation/010Alma_Online_Help_(English)/050Administration/030User_Management/010Managing_Users#Deleting_Users

Ex Libris. (n.d.). *Configuring User Deletion*. Ex Libris Knowledge Center. Retrieved July 5, 2022, from https://knowledge.exlibrisgroup.com/Alma/Product_Documentation/010Alma_Online_Help_(English)/050Administration/040Configuring_User_Management/100Configuring_Delete_User_Policy_Settings

Ex Libris. (n.d.). *Creating a New Report*. Ex Libris Knowledge Center. Retrieved August 9, 2023, from https://knowledge.exlibrisgroup.com/Alma/Product_Documentation/010Alma_Online_Help_(English)/080Analytics/010Introduction/The_Basics_of_Working_with_Analytics/050Creating_a_New_Report#Creating_Advanced_Custom_Reports

Ex Libris. (n.d.). *General Terminology*. Ex Libris Knowledge Center. Retrieved July 5, 2022, from https://knowledge.exlibrisgroup.com/Alma/Product_Documentation/010Alma_Online_Help_(English)/080Analytics/010Introduction/General_Terminology

Ex Libris. (n.d.). *Shared Dimensions*. Ex Libris Knowledge Center. Retrieved July 5, 2022, from https://knowledge.exlibrisgroup.com/Alma/Product_Documentation/010Alma_Online_Help_(English)/080Analytics/080Shared_Dimensions

Ex Libris. (n.d.). *Accessing Analytics*. Introducing Alma Analytics. Retrieved July 5, 2022, from http://exl-edu.com/01_Alma/Analytics/Introducing_Alma_Analytics/#/lessons/4YhGYeohCmxN_3SUIiXi9EE-4Wt4q4qo

Ex Libris. (n.d.). *Anonymizing Analytics Report Details*. Ex Libris Knowledge Center. Retrieved July 5, 2022, from https://knowledge.exlibrisgroup.com/Alma/Product_Documentation/010Alma_Online_Help_(English)/080Analytics/010Introduction/The_Basics_of_Working_with_Analytics/Anonymizing_Alma_Analytics_Report_Details

Florida Legislature. (n.d.). *The 2021 Florida Statutes Title XIX Chapter 286*. Retrieved July 5, 2022, from http://www.leg.state.fl.us/statutes/index.cfm?App_mode=Display_Statute&URL=0200-0299/0286/0286ContentsIndex.html&StatuteYear=2012&Title=-%3E2012-%3EChapter%20286

Wikipedia. (2022, June 16). *Ex Libris Group*. Retrieved July 5, 2022, from https://en.wikipedia.org/wiki/Ex_Libris_Group

BIG DATA AT THE BIG HOUSE
What Do University of Michigan Patrons Think About Their Library Data?

Delaney Jorgensen, Zoe Garden, and Craig Smith

INTRODUCTION

Data analytics (or, simply, analytics) is a practice that typically involves organizing, processing, joining, analyzing, and interpreting data to reveal meaningful patterns and insights (Horváth et al., 2018). Analytics often uses large amounts of data (sometimes termed "big data"), and the data sources for analytics tend to be ever-growing in this digital age. Institutions employ analytics across a wide range of contexts. For example, marketing firms may use analytics to predict future consumer preferences and behavior based on data representing millions of past consumer behaviors. Another example comes from medicine, where analytics can design personalized preventative care based on modeling the past characteristics, behaviors, conditions, and outcomes of millions of patients (Ristevski & Chen, 2018).

Educational institutions have also embraced the use of analytics. For example, many colleges and universities build prediction models using existing student data to identify students at elevated risk for adverse academic outcomes (Namoun & Alshanqiti, 2020). Analytics methods can also assess the impact of activities and interventions on college and university campuses (e.g., various forms of instruction). In addition to using analytics at the central campus level, many academic institutions also engage in analytics at the unit or department levels. *Library analytics* incorporates analytics into unit-level assessment and planning.

Library Analytics

Libraries have adopted analytics for a wide range of purposes, such as demonstrating the impact of library instruction on student outcomes, such as GPA and retention (e.g., Gaha et al., 2018; Murray et al., 2016). The publication *The Value of Academic Libraries: A Comprehensive Research Review and Report* (Oakleaf, 2010) inspired many libraries to learn about the possible value analytics can bring to their work. Higher education institutions have been setting newer and more rigorous expectations for the performance of their academic units. In many cases, positive unit-level progress or impact must be demonstrated with data; for example, academic libraries can use analytics to provide positive impact data when making budget requests.

The use of analytics by academic libraries has been met with some criticism, however. Some key critiques involve concerns about the ethical and privacy issues that arise when libraries retain patron data and engage in analytics (e.g., Jones et al., 2020a). Further, when libraries do publish their analytics findings, statistically significant results are typically driven by large sample sizes and characterized by effect sizes so small as to be nearly null (Robertshaw & Asher, 2019). In addition, these findings of questionable practical significance are often further weakened by the lack of controls for other possible explanatory variables (such as motivation, which can drive both student library use and student academic performance). Thus, there is a tension between the loss of privacy that accompanies the storage of patron data and retaining patron data for analytics studies that do not typically bear useful fruit.

There are potential positive uses of big data by libraries, though these are not typically discussed in the context of library analytics. For example, libraries with diversity and inclusion goals could use analytics methods to seek insights into which groups on campus are adequately reached by various library services and which groups are not.

The Current Research

The University of Michigan Ann Arbor (U-M) central library system has been considering using library analytics to better understand how students (and other patrons) connect with the library's various resources. Before using analytics for such a purpose, there was a desire to understand how patrons on U-M's campus felt about the library retaining patron data and using it in analytics models. Gaining such an understanding was the goal of the present study.

As we created our research design, we benefited from the ongoing work of the Data Doubles research project (Jones et al., 2019a). The Data Doubles project has explored undergraduate student perspectives on data privacy in academic libraries via interviews, multi-institution student surveys, and scenario-based focus groups (Jones et al., 2020b). In their recent student survey (Asher et al., 2022), the Data Doubles team found that nearly all undergraduate respondents valued general data privacy, especially to prevent intrusions in their lives. They also found that more than half of their student respondents assumed some level of retention and use of their library data, such as what library materials and services students have accessed. This survey data aligns with the student interviews conducted by the Data Doubles team, in which students were quite aware that their libraries tracked information about things like physical materials usage (Jones et al., 2019b).

Nonetheless, undergraduates were generally less aware of other types of student data that universities and libraries collect, retain, and utilize (Jones et al., 2020b). In the Data Doubles interviews, most students held positive views about how libraries could use patron data (e.g., to refine services, to provide personalized services, etc.) but held deep privacy concerns about other types of data being available to university units such as libraries (e.g., health data, grades). Interviewees were also less positive about their library data being shared with non-university entities.

Most respondents to the Data Doubles survey believed that their financial and medical data were completely private, whereas most did not assume this about their library data. The study also found that students are much more comfortable with their universities retaining and using their library data, compared to collecting their financial and health records. Thus, trust in academic libraries is relatively high among undergraduate students; this fits with other data showing that library staff are highly trusted relative to most professions (Ipsos MORI, 2021; Lockwood & Ritter, 2016). However, students also set clear boundaries in relation to this trust, and many expressed a desire to have their consent requested about the collection, retention, and use of student data.

Based on a review of the current literature, including the work of the Data Doubles project, we developed the following research questions to guide the current investigation:

- What kind of data do university library patrons expect the library to store about library users, and what thoughts, feelings, and concerns do library patrons experience when they learn about actual data collection practices?
- How would library patrons want to see patron-related library data protected, and how would patrons like—or not like—the library to use the data it retains?
- What levels of trust do patrons feel about the storage of their personal data by the library and by other institutions (e.g., the larger university, corporations, etc.)?
- How do patrons feel about the specific idea of the library using patron data in analytics models (e.g., models used to generate insights into past and future patron behavior)?

We were interested in whether we would surface findings similar to those found by the Data Doubles project, especially as (a) we are not affiliated with that research group, and (b) we included two groups other than undergraduates (graduate students and faculty members). We decided to use interviews and focus groups in order to first establish the range of local student and faculty views on our research questions. By initially collecting qualitative data, our team has set the stage for the questions and response options that could populate a future survey, administered to larger numbers of students and faculty.

METHODS

Participants

Since undergraduate students are often the focus of library analytics studies (Oakleaf et al., 2017), we decided to begin the data collection process by conducting interviews with undergraduate students. After completing 11 interviews with undergraduates, we used a related methodology—focus groups—to pose similar questions to graduate students and faculty members.

The interviews with undergraduate students and the three focus groups were conducted by two members of our research team (D.J. and Z.G.), who were undergraduate students themselves during much of our data collection phase. We emailed invitations directly to a pool of 172 potential participants. The research team contacted an equal number of freshmen, sophomores, juniors, and seniors, and we oversampled from groups of students who have traditionally been underrepresented on university campuses (Black, African-American, Latinx, and Indigenous students). The University's Data Warehouse was used to identify many of our invitees; the Data Warehouse is a collection of data sources that support the business of the university, such as payroll records, student progress tracking, HR records, and financials. Those whose contact information was obtained from the Data Warehouse were reached with a "cold call" email. This list of students was obtained by semi-random sampling from the list of active undergraduates, with some planned oversampling from groups of students who have traditionally been underrepresented on university campuses (Black, African-American, Latinx, and Indigenous students). The Data Warehouse was helpful in this effort, since it captures data on class standing and race. A smaller group of undergraduates were invited from a list of students who had previously agreed to be contacted about library studies (thus, this part of our sampling approach was not random). Relatively even numbers of undergraduate participants came from both of the invitation lists described here.

Interested students were invited to participate in a single Zoom interview for a maximum of one hour. (Zoom was used due to concerns about face-to-face meetings during the COVID-19 pandemic.) Consent for both the interview and recording was obtained before each interview, and interviewees had the choice of having their cameras on or off. Our group of 11 undergraduate participants contained one freshman, six sophomores, and four juniors studying STEM fields, social sciences, and the arts and humanities. Two students identified as white, one identified as Black, five identified as Hispanic/Latinx, two identified as Asian, and one student identified as multiracial (Black and Hispanic/Latinx). While most participants were from the United States, we did have participants from South Asia and the Caribbean. We lacked diversity regarding the gender identities of our participants; nine out of 11 identified as female.

Our graduate student and faculty focus group participants were recruited in the same way (i.e., via the generation of a "cold call" list combined with the use of an existing list of those interested in helping with library studies). Graduate students and faculty came from STEM fields, social sciences, and arts and humanities. Though slightly less racially/ethnically diverse than the undergraduate group, the focus groups did include Black and Latinx participants and some international representation (from Eastern Europe). Four of the 12 focus group participants identified as male, and eight identified as female.

Participant recruitment practices and all other aspects of our research were reviewed by the Institutional Review Board at the University of Michigan, Ann Arbor (HUM00190292).

Question Protocol and Procedure

The research team first created overarching research questions (reviewed in the Introduction) to formulate the specific questions that participants answered during the interviews and focus groups. (Please see the Appendix for the full text of our interview and focus group questions.)

The interview and focus group questions were arranged in conceptual groups and asked in a purposeful order. Participants entered the discussions with no required background knowledge of library data collection or analytics. Therefore, at times we provided some necessary information (e.g., defining analytics) before asking questions to ensure a similar level of understanding among all participants.

Data Processing

Data from the 11 interviews were stored in three ways: notes taken during the interviews, verbatim interview transcripts, and audio (and, in some cases, video) recordings of the discussions. While moving from raw data to the data we report in the Results section, we relied heavily on our interview notes and transcripts. We employed a grounded, inductive approach to the data, seeking themes that emerged in the conversations. A grounded process involves seeking themes in the data without using an existing theoretical framework; instead, themes and theory are derived from the data themselves (e.g., Charmaz, 2003; Urquhart, 2013).

The initial step in our data coding process involved the research team repeatedly reading and discussing the raw interview notes and transcripts. In these conversations, the team made notes about essential themes in response to each of the questions that yielded rich data.

After becoming very familiar with the data we had collected and generating an initial set of themes, we created a provisional coding scheme for each substantive interview question. The team then reviewed the interview notes and transcripts again and adjusted the coding systems for places where the initial schemes failed to capture essential themes. We arrived at coding schemes for each substantive question, and these are presented in the Appendix.

Two research team members (Z.G. and D.J.) then independently used the coding system to code all of the interview data. Following this initial round of coding, the two sets of codes were compared. For each coder, there were 792 opportunities to either apply a code or not during the coding process (based on the number of interviewees, interview questions, and possible codes for those questions). We used Cohen's kappa as a measure of inter-rater reliability. Reliability across all of the codes was good (kappa = .80). Discrepancies in coding were then reviewed and, in all cases, were resolved quickly through discussion. A similar approach was used for coding the focus group data, but additional attention was paid to other issues that emerged in group settings (levels of agreement and disagreement). The themes that emerged from the coding process form the basis of our reporting in the Results section below.

RESULTS

Previous Knowledge of Library Data Collection

When asked about what data they believed the U-M Library was already collecting about patrons, six out of 11 undergraduate interviewees identified book checkouts as a source of retained data that captured personal information like name, student ID, checkout location, etc. An equal number of participants also assumed that their demographic data would be collected through library systems, including their gender, race, nationality, class standing, and significant area of study. The most common data that undergraduates anticipated the library would retain were related to the online resources available through the U-M Library, with seven of 11 participants identifying online databases and resources (e.g., journal access) as areas where patron data would be retained.

Each focus group consisted of four participants; two of the groups included four graduate students each, and a third focus group contained four faculty members. The majority of participants in the focus group portion of the study predicted similar forms of data collection, such as patron name, ID number, and information on the materials accessed. A few even anticipated some of the more discreet forms of data collection, such as logging information, length of session, and IP addresses/location tracking. More faculty member participants than graduate students predicted these forms of data collection, with three of four participants expecting some form of patron data beyond directory information and information on library materials. However, at least one graduate student in each focus group already anticipated that the library would be collecting data on things like IP addresses and clicks on library webpages. As such, both faculty members and graduate students collectively predicted more depth of the library's data collection practices compared to their undergraduate counterparts.

Thoughts and Feelings on Actual Library Data Collection

Before asking further questions about library data, the interviewers shared information about the data the U-M Library retains about patrons. This information is summarized on a website provided by the University's Information and Technology Services. The types of patron data collected include patron profile information, information on the use of library materials and services, logging information (e.g., type of browser, IP address, timestamp, etc.), and information on who has received library instruction. After participants were presented with this information on library data collection practices, they were asked for their initial reactions.

Six out of 11 undergraduate participants correctly anticipated the level of data collection from the U-M Library. However, other undergraduates (three of 11) were surprised at the amount of data collected or thought that some data collected by the library seemed unnecessary.

When asked whether they trusted the library to be responsible for the data collected on patrons, seven of 11 undergraduate participants expressed no concern. In addition, six of 11 expressly stated that they trusted the U-M Library to be responsible with their data, and five of 11 extended this trust to the University of Michigan at large. However, three out of 11 participants were concerned at some level with the library's data management responsibilities.

After assessing the level of trust participants held concerning the library's ability to manage patron data responsibly, the researchers asked whether undergraduates could identify some way(s) that the library could potentially use the data it collects to do something useful for them and their peers. Undergraduate answers varied for this question, as shown in Figure 1.

In the focus groups, graduate students and faculty had similar reactions to the undergraduates (Figure 2). While it was typical for one or, in the case of the second graduate student group, two participants to mention concerns or express surprise, the majority of participants were not highly concerned upon learning what types of data the library collects. We note, however, that nearly double the number of graduate students expressed surprise at the amount of data collected by the library than their faculty counterparts, which could influence the library's strategy concerning future communications with students, specifically, regarding the data they generate as patrons of the library system.

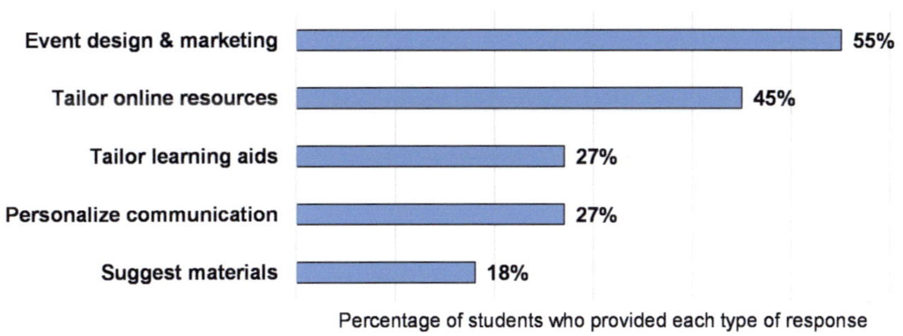

Figure 1. Undergraduate students' ideas about how the library could use patron data in helpful ways.

Figure 2. An example of the range of graduate student and faculty reactions when asked about the library's data collection practices.

Nearly all focus group participants expressed some degree of trust in the library to responsibly manage the data collected on patrons. Many cited a long relationship with the library without any issues of data misuse. Other participants noted that the type of data the library collected seemed banal and non-sensitive, particularly if the data were kept de-identified. Both faculty and graduate students mentioned trust in the library as a reason to accept and trust data collection, with graduate students mentioning this trust slightly more often than faculty members. In the graduate student focus groups, two of the four participants in each group noted some sort of concern related to their trust in the library. In the faculty focus group, three of the four participants noted a concern with trust. However, most concerns noted by faculty members were broad concerns with data misuse across institutions and not specific to the library (i.e., data selling, large hacks, etc.). It was common for all groups of participants to have learned any background knowledge about big data and analytics from large companies like Google, Facebook, and Amazon. They, therefore, did not always differentiate between those companies' analytics practices and what the library may potentially use analytics for at the institutional level.

Regarding library data being used for something useful for patrons, graduate student and faculty responses varied significantly and were quite different from the responses offered by undergraduate students in the interviews. Most graduate student participants shared an interest in receiving tailored recommendations, notifications on new publications in their fields of interest, and improving access to databases (for example, using student data to inform database subscriptions or giving students alerts when new databases become available).

Faculty members expressed more concern with the library using the data it collects to recommend other resources or campus events, with three out of four emphasizing that opt-in consent would be necessary before beginning any sort of recommendation system. Some graduate students also encouraged opt-in consent before any use of these analytics-related practices. Undergraduates, by contrast, more often mentioned potential benefits regarding tailored notices about library programming and campus events.

Thoughts and Feelings About Learning Analytics

Next, in our interviews and focus groups, we explicitly addressed the library's potential use of analytics. First, a research team member described analytics and gave examples of what the methodology could potentially be used for. Then, participants were asked how they felt about the potential for the library to use analytics methods with patron data. The majority of undergraduate interviewees (seven of 11) were in favor of library analytics. An equal number of participants had no pressing concerns. Four of 11 undergraduates expressed some type of concern, including concerns about data privacy, the retention of identifiers in the data, biases in analytics models that could negatively impact some historically marginalized groups, and that data collection would replace honest and direct communication with students.

Many positives about library analytics were identified in both graduate student focus groups. Graduate students identified library analytics as an opportunity to reduce hurdles in the research process, for example, by suggesting materials and connections to other research areas or using analytics to improve library resources and user experiences. Faculty members had similar observations about using analytics to improve patrons' experience conducting research on campus. However, some faculty cautioned that large amounts of data could have adverse effects if not handled with good intent. Compared to the undergraduate and graduate students, the faculty members tended to consider how data collection would impact all patrons on campus, while the graduate student groups tended to view how it would impact individual experiences within their respective groups.

When identifying potential negatives for library analytic practices, the answers differed slightly between graduate students and faculty (Figure 3). Graduate student participants were more inclined to think that patron data could be used in library analytics as long as identifiable information is protected. The main concerns identified by graduate students included (a) scholarly/academic recommendations, which could discourage student research from expanding beyond recommended materials, (b) the library possibly overstepping boundaries, influencing student behavior instead of simply being a source of information, and (c) diversity concerns about the white-majority campus community leading predictive technologies to favor certain perspectives and resources over others. Faculty participants encouraged the library to continue building physical collections, as use of these materials is associated with fewer data being collected on patrons (as opposed, for example, to the data collected when patrons use e-books). When thinking about the tension between library data collection and comfortable use of the library, one faculty member said, "People tend to be discreet about their information, but online

Figure 3. An example of the range of graduate student and faculty reactions when asked about the positives and negatives related to library analytics.

it is harder to monitor. We want to encourage people to seek out information and reliable information through the library, which requires some data privacy. We should also protect library data from politicians for any use. One of the downsides of moving library materials online is that you have to submit to data tracking, unlike a physical book checkout. It could limit access instead of helping it." Faculty members also highlighted the importance of protecting the identities of those using sensitive library materials (e.g., patron and login information) and protecting data from outside access. In summary, the data itself was not overly concerning to faculty, but how the data are protected and used was of considerable importance.

Thoughts on Transparency and Institutions

After discussing data collection and learning analytics, the line of questioning shifted to a discussion around trust, data privacy, and institutional transparency.

First, the researchers asked undergraduate interviewees if there were any types of data the library should protect anyone from accessing, even those performing assessment and research. The most common answers among undergraduates were that identifiable information should be protected (five of 11 students) and that any location-tracking data should remain confidential (four of 11). Other undergraduate students expressed that sensitive demographic details—for example, citizenship status—should be protected (three of 11), financial information should remain private (two of 11), and that information should not be shared with third parties (two of 11). We note that four of the 11 undergraduates expressed no substantial concern about the library sharing patron data.

Next, our research team wanted to learn more about what undergraduate students expect regarding the library's communication with student patrons. How, in other words, could the library be most transparent with students about data collection and use while not overwhelming student inboxes? Again, student opinion varied greatly on this question, as shown in Figure 4.

The most common preference, expressed by four of 11 undergraduates, was for the library to summarize its data collection practices in a periodic email (e.g., once a semester) to keep students up to date on how their data

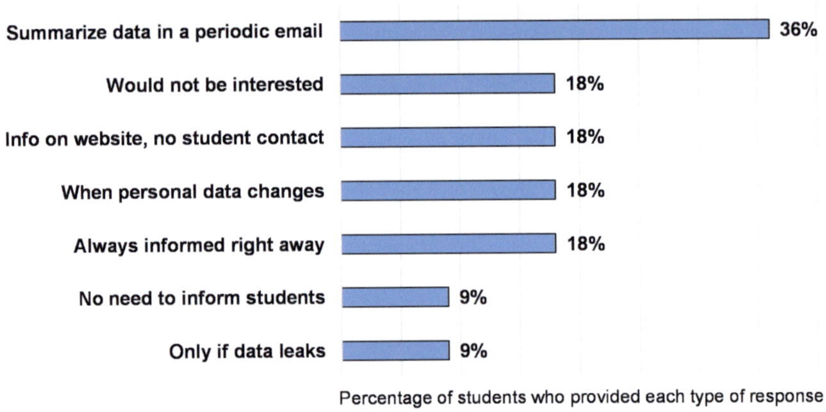

Figure 4. The range of undergraduate students' preferences about data- and privacy-related communications from the library.

is being retained, protected, and used. However, some students wished to be informed right away about any changes to library data policies. At the same time, other students felt there was no need for the library to educate students about their data-related practices.

Finally, undergraduates were asked about whether the library should seek permission for collecting and using patron data. Five of the 11 undergraduate participants expressed that there should be some mechanism to gain student authorization. Another five undergraduates responded that they had no personal concerns about data being collected without their permission. Smaller groups of undergraduate participants were not personally concerned but understood why other students might be (three of 11), felt that authorization would not change the way that students interacted with library resources (two of 11), or expected data collection from the library and therefore did not find authorization for collection necessary (two of 11).

The majority of graduate students favored an opt-in/opt-out method for data collection, while some graduate students suggested email communication, an orientation, or a message only sent out once a year. Faculty members highlighted that they would appreciate being told about the patron data being collected, with the favored method being information shared during orientation or in a once-a-year message.

DISCUSSION

Summary of Key Findings

Among both students and faculty, there were varying levels of comfort with library analytics, ranging from pro-analytics stances to strong concerns about these methods of utilizing patron data. Many participants fell somewhere in the middle. Another area where there was a great deal of variability was in participants' preferences regarding how the U-M Library communicates with its patrons—and obtains consent from them—regarding data collection. Many of the participants who expressed strong concerns with library analytics were also concerned more about general data privacy issues (e.g., discomfort with the data collection practices of large companies like Google, Facebook, and Amazon). If the library does decide to employ analytics in the future, it would be useful to differentiate the sorts of analytics that the library plans to conduct from how for-profit organizations utilize user data and analytics.

Importantly, most participants in the study expressed an overall feeling of resignation to data collection as a consequence of living in the digital age. However, oftentimes the *purpose* of this data collection was unclear to participants. This problem could be addressed by increasing communication with patrons on the topic of library data collection.

While some topics, like communication with patrons, may require further study, the findings from the interviews and focus groups offer a better understanding of how university community members, both students and faculty, view themselves in relation to the services they use on campus. Despite the passive connotation of the aforesaid "resignation" to collecting data, nearly all participants could think of at least one example of how the library could do something useful for them with the data it collects. Most participants were either in favor or did not have a strong opinion, suggesting that opinions among the university community may be generally positive with regard to analytics specifically aimed at improving library services. Participants broadly agreed that identifiable information should be kept private and secured from any outside sources, though responses on the level and amount of data to be kept private or, sometimes, not collected at all did vary somewhat.

Relation to Previous Findings

During the beginning stages of our project, the Data Doubles resources (https://datadoubles.org) acted as a useful reference point. In the end, many of our findings overlapped with the Data Doubles findings, and we also surfaced some unique themes. Like the Data Doubles project (e.g., Asher et al., 2022), our study also found that students (and faculty members) have strong concerns about data privacy in general, that many patrons expect some degree of data collection by libraries, and that many patrons are resigned and/or comfortable with data collection by their campus library. As in some of the Data Doubles studies (e.g., Jones at al., 2019b), we also found that students were not aware of all the types of data that were being captured about them by the library (though faculty members were more savvy), but that many patrons generally trusted the library to store and conduct analyses with the data.

Our interviews and focus groups also surfaced some difficult issues about data collection and analytics. First, many students and faculty members wanted some form of communication from the library about their data, but while some patrons looked favorably on opt-in/opt-out choices being offered by the library, some patrons said they are already overloaded by university communications. A related finding is that a notable minority of patrons held very strong negative views of library data collection; balancing the needs of these patrons with plans for library analytics could prove challenging. Finally, multiple participants in our research noted concerns about biases in analytics models that could cause harm or disadvantage to groups that have been underrepresented and/or marginalized; this issue of bias in algorithms and models must also be tackled by libraries seeking to use patron data in a responsible manner.

Reflections and Next Steps

The diversity of our participants allowed us to emphasize the privacy concerns of people from groups traditionally marginalized on college and university campuses. Another strength of our study was that, despite the small number of participants, we obtained rich variability in the responses to our questions while achieving a decent degree of thematic saturation (Morse, 1995).

We also acknowledge some limitations to our work. A key limitation was the small group of participants we spoke with in interviews and focus groups. It is possible that if we had heard from a larger group of people and had achieved more diversity in factors such as gender identity, disability status, and political orientation, additional perspectives, ideas, and concerns would have risen to the surface. To address these shortcomings, we plan to conduct a survey on library data and analytics that will allow us to reach many more campus stakeholders than is possible in a purely qualitative study. The lessons learned from the present study, however, will greatly inform the design of the future survey.

Based on the results of our study, there are steps that the U-M Library can take to ensure a stronger commitment to its patrons' data privacy. While data analytics models used by corporations like Google and Amazon are more nefarious in terms of their respect for privacy and user consent, there is at least an established understanding of *why* these companies collect data on their users. With regard to library data, our study's participants talked about how the justifications for collecting certain types of data seem unclear or vague. We recommend that the library communicate directly with patrons, explaining *why* the library collects and retains patron data and what that data is used for.

The level of communication that participants wished to receive from the library varied a great deal, however. Because of this variation and the concerns raised throughout our interviews and focus group conversations, we recommend that the library implement an "opt-in" model of obtaining consent for collecting data on patrons. This strategy is consistent with standards for public libraries across the United States; the American Library Association urges libraries to limit their collection of personally identifiable data and to avoid unnecessary data collection whenever possible (Resolution on the Retention of Library Usage Records, 2006). When asking for opt-in consent, the library should provide enough information for patrons to understand (a) what data are being collected, (b) what these data will be used for, and (c) how the data are protected.

Our research questions were informed by the tension between some potentially positive uses of library analytics and the erosion of patron privacy necessary to engage in the methodology. By directly exploring questions related to this with student and faculty participants, we highlight the nuanced and variable opinions across our campus community, and underscore the necessity of addressing data-related privacy and communication concerns. University libraries, known for providing unrestricted access to information for their communities, should proceed with caution before retaining and using sensitive patron data. We encourage continued research on this topic so that library systems can make the best, most informed decisions regarding the balance between library data use and patron privacy.

REFERENCES

Asher, A., Briney, K. A., Jones, K. M. L., Regalado, M., Perry, M. R., Goben, A., Smale, M. A., & Salo, D. (2022). Questions of trust: A survey of student expectations and perspectives on library learning analytics. *Library Quarterly, 92*(2), 151–171. https://doi.org/10.1086/718605

Charmaz, K. (2003). Grounded theory. In J. A. Smith (Ed.), *Qualitative psychology: A practical guide to research methods* (pp. 81–110). Sage Publications, Inc.

Gaha, U., Hinnefeld, S., & Pellegrino, C. (2018). The academic library's contribution to student success: Library instruction and GPA. *College & Research Libraries, 79*(6), 737–746. https://doi.org/10.5860/crl.79.6.737

Horváth, T., De Carvalho, A., & Mendes Moreira, J. (2018). *A general introduction to data analytics*. John Wiley & Sons.

Ipsos MORI. (2021). Ipsos MORI Veracity Index 2021: Trust in professions survey. Available from: https://www.ipsos.com/sites/default/files/ct/news/documents/2021-12/Veracity%20index%202021%20-%20topline%20v1_PUBLIC.pdf

Jones, K. M. L., Asher, A., Briney, K., Goben, A. H., Perry, M., Regalado, M., Salo, D., & Smale, M. (2019a). Data Doubles. https://doi.org/10.17605/OSF.IO/D7F3G

Jones, K. M. L., Perry, M. R., Goben, A., Asher, A., Briney, K. A., Robertshaw, M. B., & Salo, D. (2019b). In their own words: Student perspectives on privacy and library participation in learning analytics initiatives. *Proceedings of the Annual Meeting of the Association of College and Research Libraries*. https://alair.ala.org/handle/11213/17656

Jones, K. M. L., Briney, K., Goben, A., Salo, D., Asher, A., & Perry, M. (2020a). A comprehensive primer to library learning analytics practices, initiatives, and privacy issues. *College & Research Libraries, 81*(3), 570–591. https://doi.org/10.5860/crl.81.3.570

Jones, K. M. L., Asher, A., Goben, A., Perry, M. R., Salo, D., Briney, K. A., & Robertshaw, M. B. (2020b). "We're being tracked at all times": Student perspectives of their privacy in relation to learning analytics in higher education. *Journal of the Association for Information Science and Technology, 71*(9), 1044–1059. https://doi.org/10.1002/asi.24358

Lockwood, B. M., & Ritter, J. (2016) Maine State Library: Trusted Professionals Survey 2016. Library Documents, Paper 101. Available from: http://digitalmaine.com/msl_docs/101

Morse, J. M. (1995). The significance of saturation. *Qualitative Health Research, 5*(2), 147–149. https://doi.org/10.1177/104973239500500201

Murray, A., Ireland, A., & Hackathorn, J. (2016). The value of academic libraries: Library services as a predictor of student retention. *College & Research Libraries, 77*(5), 631–642. https://doi.org/10.5860/crl.77.5.631

Namoun, A., & Alshanqiti, A. (2020). Predicting student performance using data mining and learning analytics techniques: A systematic literature review. *Applied Sciences, 11*(1), 237. https://doi.org/10.3390/app11010237

Oakleaf, M. (2010). Value of Academic Libraries Report | ACRL Value of Academic Libraries. In *Association of College and Research Libraries*. Association of College and Research Libraries. https://acrl.ala.org/value/?page_id=21

Oakleaf, M., Walter, S., & Brown, M. (2017). *The Academic Library and the Promise of NGDLE*. EDUCAUSE Review. https://er.educause.edu/articles/2017/8/the-academic-library-and-the-promise-of-ngdle

Resolution on the Retention of Library Usage Records. (2006). B.8.5.4 - Retention of Library Records. *Alair.ala.org*. https://alair.ala.org/handle/11213/1594

Ristevski, B., & Chen, M. (2018). Big data analytics in medicine and healthcare. *Journal of Integrative Bioinformatics, 15*(3). https://doi.org/10.1515/jib-2017-0030

Robertshaw, M. B., & Asher, A. (2019). Unethical numbers? A meta-analysis of library learning analytics studies. *Library Trends, 68*(1), 76–101. https://doi.org/10.1353/lib.2019.0031

Urquhart, C. (2013). *Grounded theory for qualitative research: A practical guide - SAGE Research Methods*. Methods.sagepub.com. https://methods.sagepub.com/book/grounded-theory-for-qualitative-research

APPENDIX

SECTION 1: INTERVIEW AND FOCUS GROUP PROTOCOL

Intro Script

INTERVIEWS:

- Intro to interviewers (and roles for this particular interview—lead vs. note taker)
- Description of study/interview process
    - o The study is exploring U-M students' thoughts and opinions on the data the library collects about its users, including students.
    - o The interview will last no longer than one hour, and you can ask to stop at any time.
    - o You will receive a $25 gift card for your participation.
    - o Participation in this study does not involve notable risks to participants.
    - o There are no right or wrong answers to any interview question. We're just interested in what you think.
    - o Results of the study may be published, but no information would be included that would identify you.
- Consent for study
    - o If they've read the form ahead of time, just see if they have questions. Then ask if they consent to participate.
- Consent to record
    - o Ask if they are okay with recording the Zoom session (and note that recordings will be deleted after the project is over).
    - o (Note that it's okay if they don't want it recorded.)

Any questions before we get started?

FOCUS GROUPS

Z.G. and D.J. introduce themselves and their role at the library.

Call on each participant to introduce themselves and respond to the following questions:

- What are your name and pronouns?
- [For grad students] What are you studying at U-M?
- [For faculty] What department do you work in at the university?
- What would you say is the main way you use the U-M Library?
- Intro to interviewers (and roles for this particular interview—lead vs. note taker)
- Description of study/focus group process
    - o The study is exploring U-M students' and faculty's thoughts and opinions on the data the library collects about its users.
    - o The focus group will last no longer than one hour, and you can ask to stop at any time.
    - o You will receive a $30 gift card for your participation.
    - o Participation in this study does not involve notable risks to participants.
    - o There are no right or wrong answers to any question. We're just interested in what you think.
    - o Results of the study may be published, but no information would be included that would identify you.
- Consent for study—Link to Consent Qualtrics
    - o See if there are any questions.
    - o Then ask if they consent to participate.
- Consent to record
    - o If someone indicated on the qualtrics form that they don't want the interview recorded, do not record the interview.
    - o If all participants indicated that they are ok with recording, acknowledge that and then start the recording.
    - o ALSO—note that recording is only used to flesh out notes and then be deleted.

Any questions before we get started?

Set a few key ground rules for the discussion

- We will monitor raised hands throughout the discussion, so please use that function when appropriate.
- If you have a comment to share, please communicate verbally with the group. If you are having connection difficulties or come up with

an answer to a previous question later in the discussion, you can also share ideas in the chat.

- You can use direct chat with Zoe or Delaney if you are having technical issues or would like to leave the focus group at any time.
- Unless a participant says something that's combative or offensive, we want to emphasize that all opinions are valid and should be respected during our conversations.
- We want all group members to participate equally in this discussion; if you know that you have been participating a lot, you can step back and give others the chance to share. We also encourage quieter participants to speak up because we value your opinion. Zoe and Delaney will help facilitate the conversation more directly if there is an imbalance.
- Everything said in this discussion is private, so we encourage you to keep people's identities and names confidential after this focus group session is complete. We will do the same in our data collection and analysis.

Ask if there are any rules others would like to add.

Opening Questions

1. What year of your studies are you in at U-M?

2. What are you studying here at U-M? [FOR FRESHMEN AND SOPH] Or if you aren't sure, what are you interested in?

3. In what ways do you currently use the U-M Library?—such as getting books, accessing full-text articles, using study spaces, meeting with library staff?
   a. [IF NOT FRESHMAN] How about before the pandemic?

Understanding of Library Data

Intro Script

When you use internet services like Facebook, Instagram, and Google, these companies collect data about you. This could be personal information like demographics, or it could be information about your behavior on the service, what types of posts you interact with, what you search, etc. Other institutions collect data too. For example, the university collects personal data on things like your family's financial background, or your demographics. They can also use digital tracing to track your location around campus; for instance, when you use your MCard to access a building.

4. When you interact with the library's spaces and resources, what kind of data do you anticipate the library is collecting about you?
    a. For book checkouts?
    b. When accessing online articles?
    c. When accessing library spaces?
    d. When meeting with a library staff member?
    e. Other situations?

Thoughts/Feelings about Library Data

Intro script: On this website, which is part of U-M's Information and Technology Services, you can see some examples of what data the library collects on you [go through the website].

5. What are your reactions to hearing about the types of data the library collects on you?

6. We're interested in your level of trust in the library, with regard to responsible data management. For example, some types of data mismanagement include data leaks, data selling, and the sharing of identifiable information. Do you have concerns about any of these, with regard to library data?

7. Do you have ideas about how the library could use the data it stores about students to do something useful for students?
    a. To improve academic experiences?
    b. To improve the campus experience, for example connecting you to events or programs?

Thoughts/Feelings about Library Analytics

Intro script: Analytics involves collecting data about individual users and their practices to make inferences about users' behavior. Companies sometimes use those inferences and predictions to suggest products or target advertising. As we noted, you also generate data when you interact with the university and library websites, buildings, and services. The library could also use the data you generate to engage in analytics. For example, the library could look at the connection between patterns of library use among students and its correlation to student GPA. Or the library could use patterns of book checkout behavior to generate recommendations for future checkouts.

INTERVIEWS

8. The library is considering using an analytics approach to data. How do you feel about this?
   a. [IF NO CONCERNS EXPRESSED]: Do you have any concerns about the library using the data for analytics projects?

FOCUS GROUPS

8a. The library is considering using an analytics approach to data. Do you see the ways that this approach to collecting data could be positive for library patrons?

8b. Do you have any concerns about the library using data for analytics projects?

Thoughts about Transparency and Protection

9. Now that you know a bit more about the types of data collected by the library, are there certain types of library data that you think the library should protect anyone from accessing (including people doing assessment and research)?
10. Do you think the library has any responsibility to actively reach out to you to inform you about the data they collect and store about you?
    a. [IF YES] How would you want this communication to take place?
    b. [IF NO] Why not?

(INTERVIEWS ONLY)

11. Social media sites and other online platforms often have "terms of service." By agreeing to these terms, users give these companies authorization to collect and possibly store data about their behavior on those sites. The library currently does not ask for students' authorization to collect their data. How do you feel about this practice?

Closing Questions

12. Are there things about the library and your data that you want to share—things we didn't cover so far?

13. Do you have any other questions, ideas, or comments?

(INTERVIEWS ONLY)

14. What is the best mailing address for us to send you your gift card?

SECTION 2: CODING SCHEMES FOR INTERVIEWS AND FOCUS GROUPS

INTERVIEWS

Q4: When you interact with the library's spaces and resources, what kind of data do you anticipate the library is collecting about you?

Coding categories used:

- Book
- Online resources
- Library spaces
- Staff member meeting
- Accessing databases
- Demographics
- Other situations

Q5: What are your reactions to hearing about the types of data the library collects on you?

Coding categories used:

- Not surprised / expected
- Explicit expression of not being concerned

- Surprised at amount of data collected
- Some and/or all of it feels invasive
- Some of it feels unnecessary
- Trusts that the library only collects what it needs to serve patrons
- Concerned / surprised about data retention
- Concern with lack of notification and/or consent
- Understands why some people may have concerns
- Concern about data shared with / held by third parties
- Concern about use of Google analytics
- Uncodable / difficult to code

Q6: We're interested in your level of trust in the library, with regard to responsible data management. For example, some types of data mismanagement include data leaks, data selling, and the sharing of identifiable information. Do you have concerns about any of these, with regard to library data?

Coding categories used:

- No concerns at all
- Mildly concerned
- Resigned to data collection
- Concerned after learning new info about library data
- Trusts library to be responsible with data
- Trusts the library more than the university as a whole
- Trust in the library is equal to trust in the university

Q7: Do you have ideas about how the library could use the data it stores about students to do something useful for students?

Coding categories used:

- Suggest materials
- Filter databases
- Expand library catalog
- Personalize communication with students
- Suggest events
- Create events around frequent student questions or student interests
- Increase access to popular materials (i.e., databases, subscriptions)
- Create aids or learning initiatives to help student learning

- Connect students to summer opportunities
- No ideas

Q8: The library is considering using an analytics approach to data. How do you feel about this?

Coding categories used:

- In favor of using analytics on student data
- Does not think they would be personally affected by analytics
- Uncertain / needs more information
- Not sure if student data is applicable to library analytics
- Concerned about data privacy
- Concerned about identifiable information
- Concerned about bias in technology for social identities
- Concerned that data collection will replace real conversations with students
- No personal concerns, but understands that other students may have data privacy concerns
- No pressing concerns

Q9: Now that you know a bit more about the types of data collected by the library, are there certain types of library data that you think the library should protect anyone from accessing (including people doing assessment and research)?

Coding categories used:

- Identifiable information should be protected
- Information should not be shared with third parties outside the university (including local, state, and federal governments)
- Location information should be protected
- Sensitive demographic information should be protected
- Financial information should be protected
- General online activity should be protected
- OK with the library sharing identifiable data
- OK with the library sharing demographic data
- Not concerned about data sharing
- Understands why other students may be concerned about data sharing
- No ideas

Q10: Do you think the library has any responsibility to actively reach out to you to inform you about the data they collect and store about you?

Coding categories used:

- Yes, students should be informed of all data collection by the library
- Yes, students should be informed when their personal data changes
- Yes, but only to summarize what's being collected periodically
- Yes, but only in the case of a data breach or leak
- The library should provide information, but does not need to actively reach out to students
- Students would not be interested in learning about their data
- The library has a right to collect data without informing students
- Favors opt-in / opt-out system of collection

Q11: The library currently does not ask for students' authorization to collect their data. How do you feel about this practice?

Coding categories used:

- Yes, the library should ask for student authorization
- Yes, but no in-depth information is necessary
- No personal concerns
- Understands why other students may be concerned
- Authorization would not change how students interact with the library
- Authorization makes students pessimistic about data collection
- Expects data collection from the library
- Was unaware that the library did not ask for authorization

Concrete suggestions for the library to implement an authorization system (# of undergraduates who mentioned each suggestion):

- Terms of service (3)
- Keep terms of service shorter than one page (1)
- Minimal communication (3)
- Model Wolverine Access' consent process (2)
- Opt-in / opt-out, and discuss with students (1)

FOCUS GROUPS

Q4: When you interact with the library's spaces and resources, what kind of data do you anticipate the library is collecting about you?

Coding categories used:

- Information on materials accessed
- Patron data
- Session information (i.e., length of session, downloads)
- Data for recommendations
- Did not know / unsure if library collects data

Q5: What are your reactions to hearing about the types of data the library collects on you?

Coding categories used:

- Surprised
- Not surprised
- Has questions
- Concerns about data collected
- Collecting more data than expected

Q6: We're interested in your level of trust in the library, with regard to responsible data management. For example, some types of data mismanagement include data leaks, data selling, and the sharing of identifiable information. Do you have concerns about any of these, with regard to library data?

Coding categories used:

- Trusts library to be responsible
- Trust in university as a whole
- Institutional framework (i.e., laws, IRB) protects data
- Data are not interesting / vulnerable enough
- Concerned in some way

Q7: Do you have ideas about how the library could use the data it stores about students to do something useful for students?

Coding categories used:

- Recommendations
- Identifying areas for further research / subfields
- Improving databases
- Troubleshooting online resources

Q8a. The library is considering using an analytics approach to data. Do you see the ways that this approach to collecting data could be positive for library patrons?

Coding categories used:

- Benefits for research
- Benefits to connect to other communities
- Beneficial for library resources / improving resources
- Beneficial for the library as a whole
- Beneficial for patrons / user experience

Q8b. Do you have any concerns about the library using data for analytics projects?

Coding categories used:

- Recommendation concerns
- Opt-in / opt-out concerns
- Overall data concerns
- Patron data concerns
- Diversity concerns
- Scholarly / academic concerns
- Library overstepping boundaries

Q9: Now that you know a bit more about the types of data collected by the library, are there certain types of library data that you think the library should protect anyone from accessing (including people doing assessment and research)?

Coding categories used:

- Protect library materials
- Protect patron information
- Protect login information
- Protect data from outside access
- No concerns

Q10: Do you think the library has any responsibility to actively reach out to you to inform you about the data they collect and store about you?

Coding categories used:

- Reach out regarding patron data
- Opt-in / opt-out

- Email message
- Library is not responsible for communication
- Library is responsible for communication
- Unsure about responsibility of library
- Patrons assume data collection by default
- Reach out once a year (offer an orientation, or send a one-time message)

CHAPTER 5
PRIVACY AND ACCESS CONTROL

Tim Lloyd

INTRODUCTION

Historically, access control in libraries was not a major source of privacy concerns. Traditional solutions, such as IP address authentication and referral URL, were anonymous by design or left decisions in the hands of users. Library vendors offered static experiences with little opportunity for personalization. And any personally identifiable information (PII) collected was typically the result of explicit decisions by users, with publishers and libraries aware of the data flowing through their systems.

Our industry is in a different place now.

The introduction of the European Union's General Data Protection Regulation (GDPR) in May 2018 changed everything. The direct impact was that every publisher with a digital presence had to pay careful attention to the data collected from users within the EU. The resulting changes in systems, processes, and workflows have typically been applied to all users because of the cost and complexity of segmenting data processing by user, and the emergence of similar laws in other jurisdictions. Indirectly, GDPR introduced a new understanding of, and emerging expectations around, data gathering and use that have informed all subsequent developments. Data privacy regulations now require us all to pay attention to PII—how we collect it, how we secure it, how we use it. And not just what we do as the organizations collecting data, but also what we allow third parties to do.

More complex single sign-on technologies often put decisions over the PII collected into the hands of technology departments, making it harder for publishers and libraries to have clear oversight of what is collected.

Growing levels of cybercrime have highlighted the importance of securing PII. In the words of a former US federal cybercrime prosecutor[1],

> I have never once met a cybercriminal who set out to gain access to a database for one purpose and only confined themselves to that one purpose once they got inside the database. It's not how criminals think. The criminal doesn't break into your home just to steal your silver; they break in to steal the silver, the jewels, the electronics, the cash, and anything else worth stealing.

And our industry has woken up to the pressing need to offer users engaging, personalized experiences. We experience this daily through the mobile apps on our phones, but over 95%[2] of academic library access still relies on anonymous authentication methods that limit opportunities for personalization.

Meeting the needs of future library patrons requires secure and privacy-preserving authentication methods that offer delivery at the point of discovery. However, while technologies like federated authentication can give libraries complete control over data sharing, they also create scope for mistakes that could lead to the unintentional release of PII. To make informed decisions, it's important that libraries understand both how these technologies can enable a more personalized access experience AND how they need to be carefully configured to protect privacy.

TRADITIONAL APPROACHES

IP Authentication

Authenticating access based on a device's IP address ("IP authentication") has been the traditional method of authenticating access to academic library resources since the 1990s. IP authentication was designed in an era where computers and access to the internet was relatively expensive. Users accessed internet resources via a set of fixed devices connected to campus networks. As a result, the list of IP addresses was generally stable and known in advance. IP addresses were inherently anonymous because they were only registered by organizations, and opportunities for personalization were extremely limited (although cookies were invented in 1994[3], it took many years for the technology to be adopted by the majority of scholarly publishers).

However, a series of trends have significantly reduced the effectiveness of IP authentication, and limited its usefulness for preserving privacy.

The link between a user's IP address and their entitlement to access library resources has increasingly weakened as users connect from devices outside campus networks. Proxying services, such as EZproxy, route the user's access through a proxy server. The service provider's access control sees only the registered IP address of the proxy server, rather than the user's underlying IP address.

However, proxying remote access is inherently unstable. Proxying relies on a predetermined configuration script, or stanza[4], to describe how to rewrite URLs in the service provider's web application and route access through the proxy server (and not direct to the vendor). Because providers continually update their web applications, many of these updates break existing scripts. Readers who subscribe to the Electronic Resources in Libraries email list (ERIL-L[5]) will be familiar with the regular drumbeat of broken proxy access.

In addition, users are more commonly discovering content using tools that are independent of the library website, such as Google and Google Scholar. Bypassing library-mediated proxy links, these users arrive directly at service provider websites on their unregistered (and therefore unauthenticated) IP addresses.

Campus IP addresses themselves are subject to change (sometimes without the knowledge of the library), often stored in a variety of formats, and pass through many hands between campus IT, the library, and service providers. An IP address audit across 150 publishers conducted by PSI (Publishers Solutions International) showed that, on average, 58% of the IP ranges held by publishers to authenticate libraries who license their content were inaccurate[6].

More recently, privacy-preserving services like Zscaler[7] and Apple's Private Relay[8] break IP authentication by deliberately anonymizing a user's IP address.

In addition, the assumption that IP addresses protect privacy is no longer true in all cases. An unintended consequence of anonymity is that users are typically forced to separately register credentials with the service provider in order to benefit from personalization (often exposing their personal email and passwords in the process). Our reliance on mobile applications to manage our lives has demonstrated the value we place on efficient experiences, and users often shun library resources that fail to offer similar levels of utility.

As a result, many academic libraries are starting to explore federated authentication as a secure and more flexible privacy-preserving alternative to IP authentication.

Username and Password

Some library resources have always relied on personalization, such as generating lists of previously accessed content or documenting achievements in an email. Username and password authentication has been a traditional solution for these resources. As with IP authentication, users are forced to register credentials directly with the service provider and the library is unable to mediate access in a privacy-preserving manner.

Referring URL

This authentication method requires the library to control access to a particular webpage. Library vendors then authenticate all users that arrive from that webpage (the "referring" URL) on the basis that access to it is managed by the library. Access is anonymous by definition. However, referring URL authentication is extremely insecure, many vendors refuse to support it, and many modern web browsers no longer provide fully qualified referring URLs (only the domain). This method only persists because it's a technically simple option for libraries with very limited budgets.

Library Cards

Many public libraries rely on validating library card numbers for authentication. In some cases, authentication simply involves matching the library card entered to a pre-registered pattern—completely insecure once the pattern is known. A more secure variant is Standard Interchange Protocol Version 2, or SIP2 for short, which is a technology that was developed and published by 3M in 1993 to support machine-to-machine authentication within a network. Simply by virtue of its availability within library systems, many public libraries adopted it for patron authentication. It works by enabling a vendor to validate library-managed credentials provided by a library patron—typically a user identifier (library card number) and pin code. However, this old-fashioned technology is clunky to implement and doesn't offer modern security features, such as built-in encryption or error codes.

FEDERATED AUTHENTICATION

Definitions

Understanding how federated authentication protects privacy requires some understanding of the roles played by the following parties involved in an authentication transaction:

- Identity Provider (IdP)—an organization that manages the identities and access rights of its users. It is able to both authenticate a user and authorize their access to services. For example, universities, schools, and research institutes. The term can also be used to describe the software application that an organization uses to manage identity and access requests from service providers.
- Service Provider (SP)—an organization that provides services. It needs to authenticate a user's identity and their entitlement to access services. For example, publishers, discovery services, and other library service providers.
- Identity Federation—an organization that operates a trust framework for the exchange of authentication assertions between its member IdPs and SPs. For example, InCommon, the UK Access Management Federation, and the OpenAthens Federation.

How Federated Authentication Works

Federated authentication is an extension of Single Sign-On (SSO) that allows you to use your organizational credentials to authenticate access to a wide variety of online resources that are provided by third parties outside your organization.

If you work for an organization, you likely use SSO daily to access applications such as email, HR tools, or payroll information. SSO allows users to login once in order to access each application, rather than having to separately login to each application every time you access it. Behind the scenes, each application is asking for authentication, but your organization's IdP software is seamlessly authenticating you. The process works smoothly because each application has an integration with the IdP software.

Federated authentication extends (or "federates") SSO functionality to third-party service providers. As there is no integration between the internal IdP and the external SP, an identity federation acts as the trusted party allowing the IdP and the SP to find and trust each other. Think of the identity federation as a directory that allows an SP to learn about an IdP and how to securely request authentication from them.

HERE'S A SIMPLE WALKTHROUGH OF THE TYPICAL AUTHENTICATION WORKFLOW:

1. The user goes directly to the SP website and clicks on a resource, such as a subscription database or paywalled journal.
2. The SP website asks the user to identify their institution. Traditionally, this requires the user to select their institution from a long list, but services like SeamlessAccess can remove this step. The user's institution represents their IdP.
3. The SP looks up this IdP in the federation directory. This confirms that the IdP is a valid organizational member of the federation and provides a URL where users can be authenticated.
4. The SP redirects the user to their IdP, using the URL provided by the federation.
5. The IdP asks the user to enter their organizational credentials, typically an email address and password. Note that the user is providing these credentials directly to their institutional IdP, and not to the SP. We'll assume that the user enters valid credentials.
6. The IdP redirects the user back to the SP, along with some metadata about the user ("attributes") that confirms their identity and their entitlement to access the SP's services.
7. The SP reviews these attributes, confirms that the user is authorized, and then redirects the user into the requested service.

If the user was already logged into their institutional IdP, then step 5 is avoided and the IdP can immediately respond to the SP. The user will be redirected to the requested service after selecting their IdP in step 2.

Advantages of Federated Authentication

Federated authentication is a stable, mature technology. One of the earliest examples in higher education was the Athens[9] project, which was conceived in 1996 following an implementation by the University of Bath in the UK. Shibboleth[10], an open source software commonly used to implement federated authentication in research and education institutions, originated in 2000 as an internal project funded by Internet2[11]. As of August 2022, c. 7,000 IdPs and 14,000 SPs authenticate users globally through identity federations in more than 70 countries around the world. And, unlike proxied access, federated authentication is unaffected by changes to SP websites.

Federated authentication is a very secure authentication method that doesn't suffer from the typical security problems, such as IP Spoofing, click-jacking, and session hijacking, of legacy access methods. The trust framework inherent in federation management ensures that you always know your counterparty, and secure encryption protects any PII shared. User credentials are only ever stored in one place, which is under the control of the institutional IdP, and are never shared with SPs. Local control also means that the underlying user directory is kept up-to-date—for example, users who leave the organization should no longer have valid credentials in the local IdP.

One of the challenges of IP authentication is that vendors who experience intellectual property theft from a particular IP address have few alternatives in the short term other than removing that IP address from the list of registered IP addresses. Unfortunately, this also prevents valid users from accessing via that IP address. In contrast, federated authentication occurs at the individual user level so one set of user credentials can be denied without impacting other users.

Local control of user credentials also means that federated authentication avoids the significant effort required to communicate and update IP addresses between campus IT, libraries, distributors, agents, and vendors.

Federated authentication offers "delivery at the point of discovery." IP authentication forces remote users to access via a proxied URL, which adds extra friction to the access workflow, and doesn't reflect how users actually behave. SPs that support federated authentication enable users to login directly at the SP website, regardless of how they got there.

Finally, and most importantly from a privacy perspective, federated authentication supports privacy-preserving access while still enabling users to personalize their experience.

Challenges of Federated Authentication

The biggest challenge that libraries face in using federated authentication is simply the cost of implementation and, to a lesser extent, maintenance.

Federated authentication is a complex technology requiring specialist skills and a steep learning curve. Institutions that don't already have a local IdP that supports federated authentication will need to invest in the software infrastructure to support it, and the skills and experience to configure, run, and maintain it. As with proxying software, many libraries will find that hosted solutions offer a much more cost-effective route to acquiring the tools and expertise needed.

ATTRIBUTES

Attributes is the term used to describe data shared in federated authentication, and "Attribute release" is the process by which that data is shared by an IdP (such as a research and education institution) with an SP (such as a library vendor) as part of the authentication process.

The format an attribute takes depends on the underlying technology. For example, Security Assertion Markup Language, or SAML for short, is the technology that underpins scholarly federated authentication, such as Shibboleth and OpenAthens. OpenID Connect is an alternative technology that supports the federated authentication used by consumer-focused services like Facebook and Google.

Attribute release is not required as part of federated authentication. However, best practice in the federation community requires the inclusion of an affiliation attribute to confirm the relationship between a user and the organization, and an entitlement attribute to confirm their authorization to access the relevant resource. Neither of these attributes contain any PII.

Here are some examples of the types of attribute that can be passed as a result of a successful user authentication:

- Affiliation attributes define the organizational association between the user and their home institution, by means of employment, membership, enrollment in an educational program, etc. For example, the user is a faculty member.
- Entitlement attributes can optionally confirm the user's right to access a given resource based on criteria previously agreed with the SP. For example, a URL for the licensing contract with the SP.
- A pseudonymous identifier can be shared that is unique to each person and for each SP, so it masks their true identity but it does enable that user to be identified by the same SP the next time they visit (but can't be used to build a pattern of usage across SPs). As a result, pseudonymous identifiers can be used to personalize a user's experience without sharing any PII.
- Personally identifiable attributes, such as your name and email address.

Attributes are important because they give both sides of the authentication transaction greater control. This control can be valuable in a variety of different ways, depending on the granularity of the information available to the IdP. For example:

- Access control: an institution can choose to make a resource available only to users who are full-time staff and students, preventing, say, alumni or contractors from access.
- Cost control: a library can limit resource access to users with a certain role or from a certain department.
- Risk control: pseudonymous identifiers allow users to benefit from personalization without exposing them to the risks (and hassle) of separately registering yet another username and password. The SP can recognize a returning pseudonymous ID and personalize that user's experience accordingly without receiving any personally identifiable data, without needing to store their email address, and without asking for a password.

Attribute release only happens after a user is authenticated. An SP can't pull attributes—they only receive what the IdP chooses to send. Because the IdP is in control, any special needs for attributes need to be agreed in advance so that attribute release can be configured appropriately.

Note that library resource access is only one of a number of valuable use cases for federated authentication. For example:

- Research collaborations involving researchers across different institutions would typically share some PII, such as a name and email address.
- Institutional workflows that require users to confirm their institutional affiliation with third parties may involve scenarios where it is appropriate to share a much broader range of user data, such as authorizing the use of institutional funds for open access publishing fees.

ENTITY CATEGORIES

To avoid IdPs having to manually configure exactly which attributes to send to each SP, configuration is managed through Entity Categories. An entity category is a metadata tag used to group entities like SPs or IdPs so that a standard set of attributes can be built and applied at the group level, rather than the individual entity level. SPs self-assert membership of one of the entity categories, signaling which attributes they need in order to work. IdPs assert support for one or more of these entity categories.

The most well-known entity category in use today is the REFEDS Research & Scholarship (or R&S) entity category. REFEDS is the Research and Education FEDerations group, which represents the global research and education identity federations. This entity category only applies to SPs that are "operated for the purpose of supporting research and scholarship interaction, collaboration or management, at least in part"[12]. It cannot be used for library access to licensed online resources.

Until 2021, there were no standards for how IdPs should release attributes for the many use cases that fall outside of the R&S entity category—such as library access to licensed resources. This has held back adoption of federated authentication by libraries, and in some cases led to accidental release of

PII where libraries have inappropriately applied the R&S entity category for library access.

In March 2021, REFEDS published two new entity categories[13] designed to address privacy concerns within the library community: Anonymous Authorization and Pseudonymous Authorization. Developed under the auspices of SeamlessAccess and after community consultation and review, these new categories provide libraries with a standard approach to protect patron privacy when users access library resources via federated authentication.

Anonymous Authorization[14] is an entity category designed for SPs that grant service access based on proof of successful authentication, which make authorization decisions based on affiliation, and which do not require any additional user attributes. The only attributes shared confirm a user's organizational affiliation and their entitlement to access the relevant resource. No user identifier or PII is shared.

Pseudonymous Authorization[15] is an entity category designed for SPs that additionally need to personalize the user experience, but don't require any PII. It releases the same attribute bundle as Anonymous Authorization with the sole addition of a pairwise user identifier. This opaque identifier is unique to each user and so can be used where the SP needs to personalize the user experience, but contains no PII and so preserves a user's real identity. It is also unique to each IdP–SP pair, and so can't be used to track a user's activity across SPs.

In November 2021, REFEDS published an additional entity category titled Personalized[16] for use by SPs that have a proven need to receive a small set of PII about their users in order to effectively provide their service to the user or to enable the user to signal their identity to other users within the service. The SP must be able to effectively demonstrate this need to their registrar and demonstrate their compliance with regulatory requirements concerning PII through a published Privacy Notice. PII such as a user's name and email address can be released as part of the attribute bundle associated with the Personalized entity category.

Note that these entity categories do not exclude the potential release of additional attributes through bilateral agreements between an IdP and an SP. In addition, any data provided directly by the user to the SP is out of scope.

SEAMLESSACCESS

SeamlessAccess[17] was created in July 2019 as a community-driven initiative to enable more seamless access to information resources, scholarly collaboration tools, and shared research infrastructure. Specifically, to deliver an access experience that is as seamless as possible, intuitive and consistent across varied systems, meets evolving expectations, and will work effectively regardless of the researcher's starting point, physical location, and preferred device.

The SeamlessAccess service builds on the existing federated authentication infrastructure to reduce access friction for users in three ways:

1. A consistent call to action that users can recognize across diverse publisher websites: "Access through your institution."
2. The service can remember your institutional affiliation across platforms.
3. Best practices around that access experience, such as the user interface and workflow.

SeamlessAccess doesn't capture or store any PII on users. The only information that SeamlessAccess records is a user's institutional affiliation, which is stored on their device in an area called local browser storage. Users can opt not to store this information, and can delete it at any point. Only the SeamlessAccess service is able to read this information, and it is shared with participating service providers for the sole purpose of simplifying your institutional login.

SeamlessAccess is also developing best practices around the use of federated authentication, such as the new entity categories referred to in the previous section, and contract language templates that reflect the implications of using federated authentication for data privacy.

RECOMMENDED PRACTICE

There are existing industry best practices for data protection. One of the most readable examples is the Data Protection Code of Conduct published by GÉANT[18], a European Research and Education network akin to Internet2 in the United States. This code of conduct aligns very closely with the American Library Association's library privacy guidelines[19] found in the ALA Code of Ethics. In brief, the code of conduct requires SPs to:

- only use attributes necessary for access;
- use as little data as possible, wherever possible;
- not do anything but provide access with this data; and
- delete or anonymize this data when it's no longer needed.

However, there are no industry best practices for data privacy. Individual organizations—both libraries and their vendors—are developing practices based on their particular skills and experience, history, traditional tools and workflows, and organizational (not user) needs. There is no consensus within libraries on what constitutes best practice, let alone across the information industry.

As a result, we have no established industry answers to questions such as:

- What role should libraries play in protecting the PII of their users? Many libraries appear to take a paternalistic approach where the user needs to be protected from themselves, and yet research[20] indicates that students are more aware than we think, and are making more sophisticated tradeoffs about their data. Is the problem simply that we're less comfortable with users making decisions that we feel aren't in their best interests?
- When should users have a say in the PII shared on their behalf by libraries? PII is routinely shared with library vendors in access workflows where users do not have effective informed consent.
- What role should libraries and publishers play in monitoring the PII they receive to ensure it's necessary, minimized, appropriate, and deleted or anonymized when no longer needed? In my experience, very few organizations have the systems to do this, let alone staff with appropriate training. And yet users and regulations are increasingly holding us accountable for what we process.

The good news is that there are some notable initiatives to start developing best practices across our industry, such as SeamlessAccess, the University of Illinois Urbana-Champaign's Licensing Privacy Project[21], and the work undertaken by the Privacy Subcommittee of ALA's Intellectual Freedom Committee to develop a Vendor and Library Privacy Community of Practice.

NEXT STEPS FOR LIBRARIES

If your library is already using federated authentication, then investigate the emerging industry standards to understand how they can help your library to protect patron privacy.

Review your library vendor service agreements to assure that the contract language is in line with your current and planned access control workflows and complies with your organization's data protection policies. Monitor the various community initiatives in this area, as they are producing practical advice and templates that can help your library to embed data privacy within vendor agreements.

If your library isn't already using federated authentication, talk to your organizational IT department about enabling support. If your organization is already using federated authentication outside the library, then there may be an existing software solution that you can leverage within the library.

If you're completely new to federated authentication, you can learn more about how it works at the SeamlessAccess Learning Center[22]. There are also emerging communities within the ALA that offer opportunities to get more involved, such as ALA Core's Federated Authentication Committee[23].

Finally, understand the risks inherent in the legacy authentication methods you are currently using, as this will inform future investment decisions.

NOTES

1. https://scholarlykitchen.sspnet.org/2018/09/18/guest-post-think-sci-hub-is-just-downloading-pdfs-think-again/
2. Based on a July 2023 analysis of a sample of 250 million authentication requests processed by LibLynx.
3. https://www.historyofinformation.com/detail.php?id=2102
4. https://help.oclc.org/Library_Management/EZproxy/EZproxy_configuration/Introduction_to_database_stanza_directives
5. https://www.eril-l.org/
6. https://www.psiregistry.org/news
7. https://www.zscaler.com/
8. https://support.apple.com/en-us/HT212614
9. https://en.wikipedia.org/wiki/OpenAthens
10. https://en.wikipedia.org/wiki/Shibboleth_(software)
11. A US Research and Education network that operates InCommon, the US identity federation. See https://internet2.edu/

12 https://refeds.org/category/research-and-scholarship
13 https://refeds.org/a/2558
14 https://refeds.org/category/anonymous
15 https://refeds.org/category/pseudonymous
16 https://refeds.org/category/personalized
17 https://seamlessaccess.org/
18 https://geant3plus.archive.geant.net/Pages/uri/dataprotection-code-of-conduct.html
19 https://www.ala.org/advocacy/privacy/guidelines
20 Example: https://er.educause.edu/articles/2021/2/data-privacy-in-higher-education-yes-students-care
21 https://publish.illinois.edu/licensingprivacy/
22 https://seamlessaccess.org/learning-center/
23 https://www.ala.org/core/member-center/sections/technology/federated-authentication-committee

CONTRIBUTOR BIOGRAPHIES

Doreen Bradley is Director of Learning Programs and Initiatives at the University of Michigan Library. She has a BA from the University of Toronto and an MILS from the University of Michigan. Doreen leads information literacy initiatives, assesses instruction, and is part of a team of 10 librarians who provide library research instruction for undergraduate students. Doreen teaches a credit-bearing digital research course and also has many years of experience in health sciences libraries. Most recently, she is involved in several analytics projects investigating the impact of library use on student and faculty success.

Cristina Colquhoun is the Instructional Design and Online Learning Librarian for Oklahoma State University Libraries. She collaborates with liaison librarians to design and create quality online information literacy instructional experiences. She has a master's degree in Educational Technology from Oklahoma State University. Cristina is passionate about the library's role in increasing educational equity and expresses this through her work in student data privacy, accessible learning design, and open educational resources (OER).

Zoe Garden is the Digital Communications Coordinator for the Deerfield Public Library in Deerfield, Illinois. She graduated in 2021 with a Bachelor of Arts in Communication and Media from the University of Michigan.

Clarke Iakovakis is Assistant Professor and Scholarly Services Librarian at Oklahoma State University. He holds an MS in Information Studies from the University of Texas and a BA in History from Texas State University. He is interested in scholarly publishing, research information management, open access, copyright, bibliometric analysis, and programming pedagogy.

Delaney Jorgensen is a graduate student at the University of Michigan School of Information, concentrating in digital archives, library science, and preservation as she works toward her Master of Science in Information. Prior to joining the School of Information, Delaney received her Bachelor of Arts from the University of Michigan in History and French & Francophone Studies. She has worked for the U-M Library since 2019 within reference, student engagement, and assessment initiatives.

Tim Lloyd is founder and CEO of LibLynx, a business specializing in Identity, Access & Analytics solutions for online resources. His career spans several decades in a variety of product development and operational roles in online publishing. Tim's particular focus is on developing innovative products and services to support online learning and research. Tim is a member of the governance committee of SeamlessAccess.org and co-chair of the outreach committee, and serves on the Project COUNTER working group on OA/unpaywalled reporting and the OA Switchboard's Message Structure working group. Tim volunteers regularly to support a variety of industry initiatives, including mentoring, and is currently co-chair of the Society for Scholarly Publishing's Annual Meeting Program Committee.

Brady D. Lund is assistant professor of information science at the University of North Texas, Department of Information Science. Brady's research primarily focuses on library technology and data studies, information ethics, scholarly communication, information behavior, and global development. He is the author of 55 peer-reviewed journal articles, 25 short papers, 5 book chapters, and 5 authored books. His most recent book is *Python for Information Professionals* (Rowman & Littlefield Publishers, 2023).

Megan Macken is the Assistant Department Head of Digital Resources and Discovery Services at Oklahoma State's Edmon Low Library where she oversees the metadata and cataloging units. She is a member of the implementation team for Experts Directory, Oklahoma State's research information management (RIM) system. Previously she worked as a digital scholarship librarian and digital archivist. She has master's degrees in Library Science and the History of Art from Indiana University.

Nikhil Motwani is a Research Professional in Digital Resources and Discovery Services at Oklahoma State's Edmon Low Library where he manages, improves, and monitors cloud infrastructure and provides support to applications hosted on the cloud for various departments. He is also a web developer and manages Edmon Low Library's website. Nikhil has an MA in Management Information Systems from Oklahoma State University.

Damith Perera is a Research Professional in Digital Resources and Discovery Services at Oklahoma State's Edmon Low Library. Damith earned his MSc from Oklahoma State University. His interests include software development, AI, Data Science, and Mixed reality.

Emily Ray is the E Resources Librarian at the Thomas G. Carpenter Library of the University of North Florida. She has presented on privacy issues at the ERL conferences and co- written an article on privacy in Serials Librarian. She also co-wrote a guide on privacy and vendors for an IMLS funded grant in 2021. In her current position, Emily licenses e-resources and sets up and manages e resource content in the LMS. From both these activities, she is familiar with privacy concerns and the interests of multiple stakeholders. Prior to working at University of North Florida, Emily has worked with metadata, acquisition and cataloging at University of Arkansas at Little Rock Library, Vassar College Libraries, Yale University Libraries and Florida International University Libraries. At these institutions she has worked with Aleph, Voyager, Millennium, Sierra, Alma ILS systems, and EDS and Primo discovery layers. A former Slavic cataloger, Emily has reading knowledge of Czech, Hungarian, and Russian.

Craig Smith is currently the Assessment Specialist, and a Senior Associate Librarian, at the University of Michigan Library. In his role in the library, he combines the assessment, institutional research, academic research, data management, and instruction skills he has gained over a variety of research, assessment, and teaching positions. His doctoral training was in developmental psychology, and he is still publishing some research in that area as well. In 2012 he founded the Living Lab program at the University of Michigan in partnership with two local museums.

Heather Staines is Senior Consultant at Delta Think and Director of Community Engagement for the OA Data Analytics Tool. Her prior roles include Head of Partnerships for the MIT Knowledge Futures Group, Director of Business Development at Hypothesis, as well as positions at Proquest, SIPX (formerly the Stanford Intellectual Property Exchange), Springer SBM, and Greenwood Publishing Group/Praeger Publishers. She is a frequent speaker and participant at industry events including the ALPSP DEIA Working Group (co-chair), the Charleston Library Conference, the STM Futurelab and Standards and Technology Executive Committee (STEC). She is President-Elect for the Society for Scholarly Publishing and a Board Member for NASIG. She has a PhD in Military and Diplomatic History from Yale University.